ORIGAMI
FOR HIM

ORIGAMI
FOR HIM

Didier Boursin

D&C
David and Charles

www.stitchcraftcreate.co.uk

Acknowledgements
I would first like to thank all those who, from near or far, helped me to develop the origami within this book.
Thank you to Eugenio Capra for the pliers
Thank you to Yoshihide Momotani for the Mach 3 plane
Thank you to Nicolas Beaudiez for the Arc ouranos plane
Thank you to Olivier Ploton for the photos
Thank you to Élodie Pichon for her choice of papers
Thank you to Laureline Sibille for the corrections
Thank you to Nina and Angelo for their advice
Thank you to Setsuko, my friend, for her good humour
And thank you also to the entire editorial team

A DAVID & CHARLES BOOK
© Dessain et Tolra/Larousse 2011

Originally published in France as *Drôles d'Origamis Pour Les Garçons*
First published in the UK and USA in 2013 by F&W Media International, Ltd

David & Charles is an imprint of F&W Media International, Ltd
Brunel House, Forde Close, Newton Abbot, TQ12 4PU, UK

F&W Media International, Ltd is a subsidiary of F+W Media, Inc
10151 Carver Road, Suite #200, Blue Ash, OH 45242, USA

A catalogue record for this book is available from the British Library.

ISBN-13: 978-1-4463-0353-5 paperback
ISBN-10: 1-4463-0353-5 paperback

Printed in China by RR Donnelley for:
F&W Media International, Ltd
Brunel House, Forde Close, Newton Abbot, TQ12 4PU, UK

10 9 8 7 6 5 4 3 2 1

Direction and editorial coordination: Colette Hanicotte
assisted by Élodie Pichon and Laureline Sibille
Editing: Joëlle Narjollet and Chantal Pagès
Graphic design: Either
Layout: ELSE
Photographs: Olivier Ploton
Cover: Véronique Laporte/Suzan Pak Poy
Production: Anne Raynaud

Photographic credits for the decorated papers:
p. 16, p. 121, p. 123 © christophe BOISSON – Fotolia.com; p. 20, p. 125, p. 127 © davidphotos – Fotolia.com; p. 22, p. 129, p. 131 © Stephen Finn – Fotolia.com; p. 24, p. 133 © cristi180884 – Fotolia.com; p. 24, p. 135 © kernel – Fotolia.com; p. 27, p. 137, p. 139 © Clivia – Fotolia.com; p. 30, p. 141, p. 143 © christophe BOISSON – Fotolia.com; p. 32, p. 145, p. 147 © renaud allemand – Fotolia.com; p. 34, p. 149, p. 151, p. 153, p. 155 © Clivia – Fotolia.com; p. 37, p. 157, p. 159 © Eric Gevaert – Fotolia.com; p. 39, p. 161, p. 163 © NLshop – Fotolia.com; p. 42, p. 165, p. 167 © Vanessa – Fotolia.com; p. 46, p. 169, p. 171 © fakegraphic – Fotolia.com; p. 4, p. 48, p. 173, p. 175 © malko – Fotolia.com; p. 50, p. 177, p. 179 © lienkie – Fotolia.com, p. 6, p. 52, p. 181, p. 183 © kristin jacobs – Fotolia.com; p. 54, p. 185, p. 187 © Atomsplitter – Fotolia.com; p. 57, p. 189 © victor zastol'skiy – Fotolia.com; p. 57, p. 191 © Richard Laschon – Fotolia.com; p. 57, p. 193 © Leysan – Fotolia.com; p. 57, p. 195 © ihor-seamless – Fotolia.com; p. 60, p. 197 © hfng – Fotolia.com; p. 60, p. 199 © handmade – Fotolia.com; p. 6, p. 60, p. 201 © NLshop – Fotolia.com; p. 62, p. 203 © Losswen – Fotolia.com; p. 62, p. 205 © Certe – Fotolia.com; p. 62, p. 207 © lekcets – Fotolia.com; p. 64, p. 209, p. 211 © Losswen – Fotolia.com; p. 45, p. 66, p. 213, p. 217 © Tolchik – Fotolia.com; p. 66, p. 215 © Roman Sigaev – Fotolia.com; p. 68, p. 219, p. 221 © hibrida13 – Fotolia.com; p. 68, p. 223, p. 225 © L.Bouvier – Fotolia.com; p. 6, p. 70, p. 227, p. 229 © pavector –Fotolia.com; p. 74, p. 231, p. 233 © matttilda – Fotolia.com; p. 2, p. 77, p. 235, p. 237 © MAXFX – Fotolia.com; p. 80, p. 239 © darren fischer – Fotolia.com; p. 80, p. 241 © sinemaslow – Fotolia.com; p. 82, p. 243, p. 245 © Anette Linnea Rasmus – Fotolia.com; p. 73, p. 84, p. 247, p. 249 © amandare – Fotolia.com; p. 6, p. 86, p. 251, p. 253 © Komvell – Fotolia.com; p. 88, p. 255, p. 257 © ELEN – Fotolia.com; p. 72, p. 82, p. 91, p. 259, p. 261 © Karin Hildebrand Lau – Fotolia.com; p. 93 © nikoniano – Fotolia.com; p. 94, p. 263, p. 265 © Elksisters Design – Fotolia.com; p. 98, p. 267, p. 269, p. 271, p. 273, p. 275 © BG Designs – Fotolia.com; p. 101, p. 277, p. 279, p. 281 © Clivia – Fotolia.com; p. 103, p. 283, p. 285, p. 287, p. 289, p. 291, p. 293, p. 295 © Igor Nazarenko – Fotolia.com; p. 106, p. 297, p. 299, p. 301, p. 303 © BG Designs – Fotolia.com; p. 96, p. 109, p. 305, p. 307, p. 309, p. 311, p. 313, p. 315, p. 317, p. 319 © Yang MingQi – Fotolia.com; p. 112, p. 321, p. 323, p. 325, p. 327, p. 329, p. 331, p. 333 © Clivia – Fotolia.com; p. 115, p. 335 © olly – Fotolia.com; p. 115, p. 337 © mettus – Fotolia.com ; p. 115, p. 339 © Vanessa – Fotolia.com; p. 118, p. 341, p. 343 © Andrey Zyk – Fotolia.com; stickers p. 345, p. 347 © art3007, © christophe BOISSON, © HPPhoto, © Inkvargus, © Sergey Konyakin, © mirabile, © ntnt, © pati, © tuna, © Jumpingsack, © darren whittingham, © Zandiepants

F+W Media publishes high quality books on a wide range of subjects.
For more great book ideas visit: www.stitchcraftcreate.co.uk

Foreword

Origami, with its universal language of fold symbols, is popular around the world. The growing interest in this art form is largely due to a handful of creative people who have succeeded in breathing new life into traditional themes. With this aim in mind, I have created a variety of paper folded models for you to choose from. Some of you will enjoy making a squadron of vintage planes and classic aircraft, others will love the sea theme and the chance to decorate the home with dolphins, sailboats and seabirds made from fantastic papers. Then again, some of you may choose to accessorize and attire with origami, while others will relish the three-dimensional puzzles I have constructed. Whatever you choose to make, these small contemporary sculptures, with their limited requirements and simple and precise moves, allow me to let you into a universe that I have created. Each and every fold has been carefully thought out and designed to ensure your maximum enjoyment. Have fun choosing your papers and conjuring up these creations. Origami is a transient art form that encourages reflection and promotes a zen-like mood. Enjoy the time you spend creating these unusual origami models and share them with your friends.

Didier Boursin

Contents

Ready for take-off _____

Kit yourself out _____

All at sea

Construction site

Folds and symbols
> Advice

Before starting, take a moment to read through Folds and symbols (pp. 8–11) and Base shapes (pp. 12–13), which explain the basic folds. These include the 'valley' fold (folded inwards and crease is at the bottom) and the 'mountain' fold (folded outwards and crease is at the top), as well as other moves and fold combinations that will come in handy.

Each fold and movement is indicated in a diagram using an arrow and two joining dots. To avoid any mistakes, make sure you know the difference between 'folding the paper' and 'marking the fold'. In the first instance, you fold the paper and keep it folded; in the second, you simply mark the fold as indicated by the double-headed arrow. If necessary refer to the subsequent diagram; this should help you to understand the previous step.

When starting out, practise making basic models, starting from a square base, using ordinary paper. The best papers to use are those that are no more than 90g in weight. Once you've had some practise, you can move on to create any of the models using the papers recommended at the end of

book. You will find that the random way in which the patterns meet the folds allows for the models to be created slightly differently each time.

The shaded diamonds indicate the difficulty level of the origami model; the more shaded diamonds, the more difficult it will be to fold. Start with the very easy models to get used to the symbols and to perfect the delicate folds and movements. Your first attempt may not be successful, but don't be discouraged; your second go is often better and paper is provided to make two versions of each model. Use one full sheet of the recommended paper unless otherwise indicated.

Very easy

Easy

Detailed

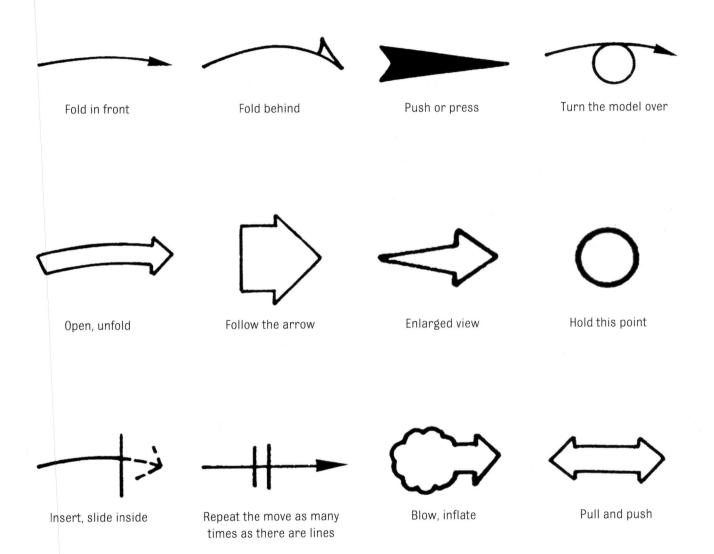

Fold in front

Fold behind

Push or press

Turn the model over

Open, unfold

Follow the arrow

Enlarged view

Hold this point

Insert, slide inside

Repeat the move as many
times as there are lines

Blow, inflate

Pull and push

Folds and symbols

> Main folds

> Valley fold

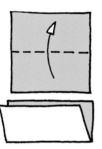

> Mountain fold

> Mark the fold

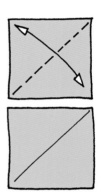

> Pleat or zigzag

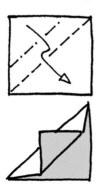

> Join the dots

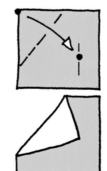

> Cut

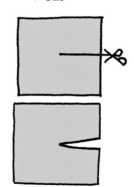

> Inside inverted fold

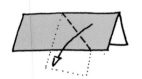 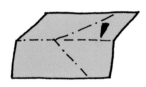 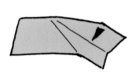

> Outside inverted fold

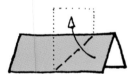 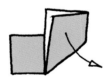 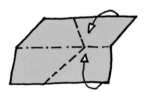 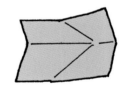

> Fold in thirds

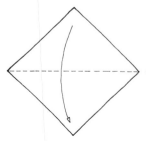   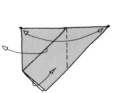 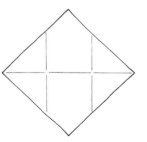

Base shapes

> Preliminary base

   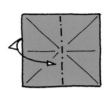

By pressing with your finger at the centre **(a)**, you obtain the Waterbomb base.

> Waterbomb base

  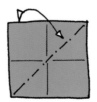

By pressing with your finger at the centre **(b)**, you obtain the Preliminary base.

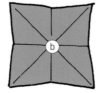 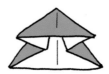 

> Bird base

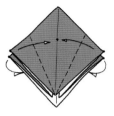  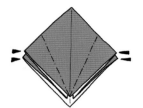 

1. Fold the lower edges onto the centre fold on both sides using a Preliminary base.

2. Unfold.

3. Push in the sides using inside inverted folds.

> Fish base

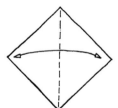 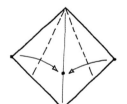  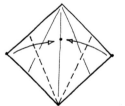

1. Mark the vertical fold.

2. Fold the upper edges onto the centre fold.

3. Unfold.

4. Fold the lower edges in the same way.

 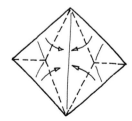  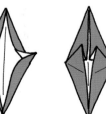

5. Unfold.

6. Refold the edges whilst simultaneously pinching the side dots.

7. Flatten, placing the dots upwards.

Ready for take-off

Mach 3

This aeroplane shoots through the sky three times faster than the speed of sound.

For recommended paper, see pp. 121 and 123

1 **Fold** the sides into the centre

2 **Fold up** the bottom edges, then fold up the tip

3 **Fold out** the tip, opening it up as shown

4 **Open out** the side flaps and the tip

5 **Join** the dots as indicated by folding up the tip

6 **Fold** the tip back down

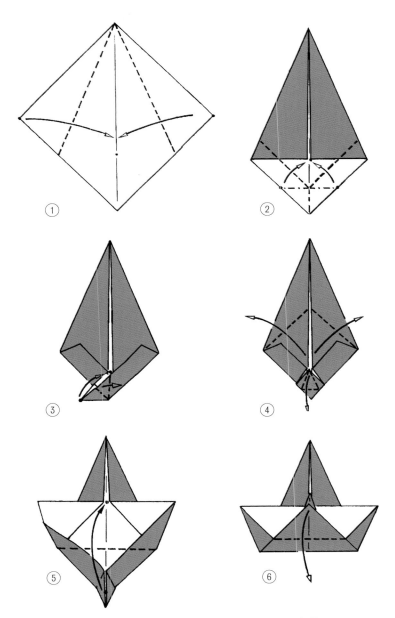

① ② ③ ④ ⑤ ⑥

7 **Fold** the side flaps into the centre

8 **Turn** over

9 **Pinch** the top

10 **Fold in** releasing the back

11 **Fold** in half behind

12 **Lift out** the wings

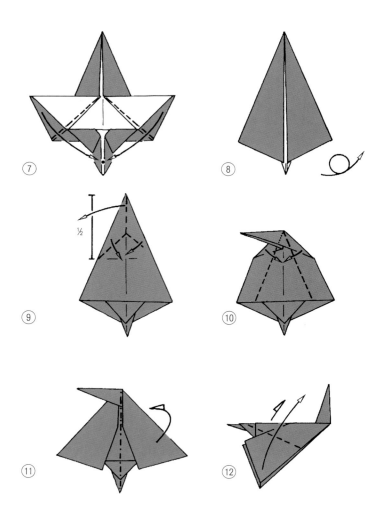

13 **Open** the pouch backwards

14 **Open** backwards (**1**), folding the wing behind (**2**)

15 **Fold** to the inside at each side on the front: at the rear fold the tail down to the centre, opening it

Details for tail

15a **Open out** the tail folds

15b **Fold down** either side of tail. Fold up the base of the wings on each side

15c **Lift up the tail folds**

16 **Sharpen** the tip, open the centre folding it in half (**1**) and lock in place by folding the sides (**2**) and (**3**)

17 **Push** into shape and open out the wings

The Mach 3 is ready to hit the clouds

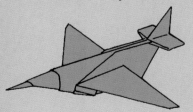

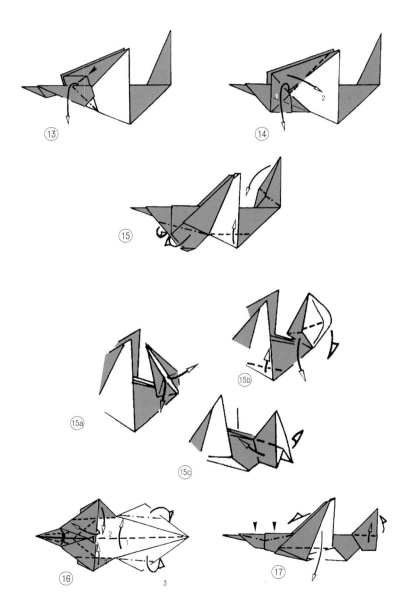

Stealth bomber

The vintage stealth bomber is designed to sneak undetected through the sky.

For recommended paper, see pp. 125 and 127

1 **Fold** in half

2 **Fold** the right side to the centre

3 **Fold** the right side in half again (**1**),
   then unfold completely (**2**)

4 **Fold** in half

5 **Fold up** the tip, as shown

6 **Fold** the right side like the left side
   following (**1**) and (**2**). Make a mountain
   fold on both sides (see p. 10)

7 **Make** an inside inverted fold (see p. 11)

   Details for wing tips

7a **Unfold** the tip and then fold the left side

7b **Fold** the left side down, then fold in half.
   Fold the other tip in the same way

8 **Fold** the plane in half

9 **Fold** the wings and make the tail at the
   back with an inside inverted fold (see
   p. 11)

10 **Prepare** to fly the completed bomber

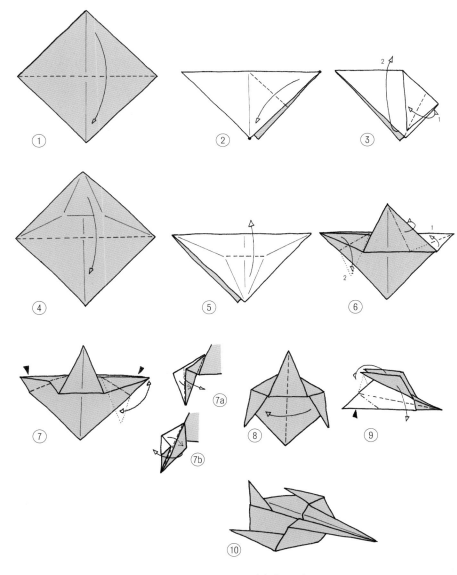

stealth bomber > **21**

Heavenly flyer

This aircraft flies so gracefully thanks to the aerodynamic design of its wings. Launch it from a great height.

For recommended paper, see pp. 129 and 131
Cut in half as marked on reverse

1 **Fold** the sides to the centre fold

2 **Fold** the sides into the centre again as shown

3 **Fold down** the tip and then turn over

4 **Fold** to join the dots

5 **Fold the tip to join** the dots, leaving the back free

6 **Mark** the folds of the fuselage and the ailerons and then fold the central axis

Adjust the wings and then hold the aircraft from underneath to launch it

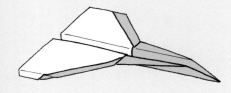

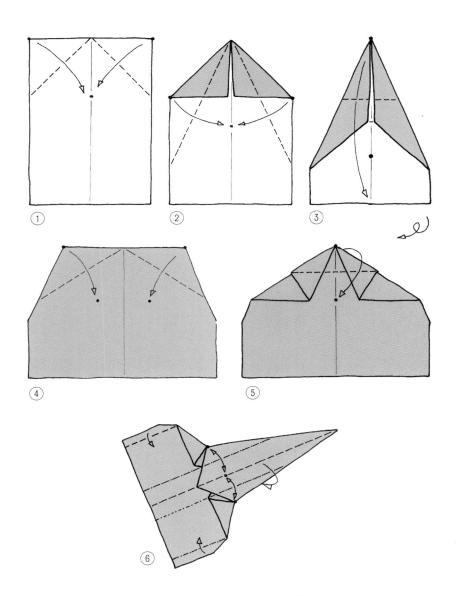

Mail plane

This utility plane is made using just half a sheet of paper. You can attach it to a wire to make an airborne ornament for your home.

For recommended paper, see pp. 133 and 135
Cut in half as marked on reverse

1   **Fold** the paper rectangle upwards as shown by the dotted line

2   **Fold** to join the dots

3   **Mark** the fold, then unfold

4   **Refold** along the folds (see waterbomb base p. 12)

5   **Check** your model is as shown, then turn over

6   **Fold** each side to the centre, then fold along the central axis

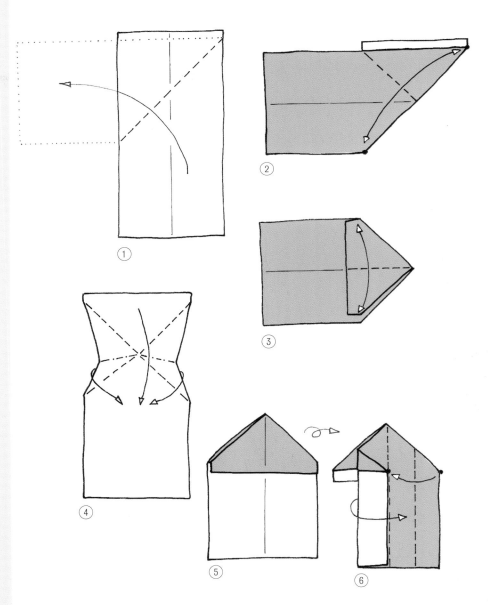

To form the tail

7 **Fold** each side along the dotted lines

8 **Mark** the fold as shown, then unfold

9 **Make** an outside inverted fold (see p. 11)

10 **Unfold** the hidden flaps

11 **Refold** the whole thing along the axis of the plane

12 **Fold** the sides to form the fuselage

13 **Fold** the end of the wings

14 **Make** any final adjustments to the aircraft to prepare for flight

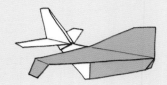

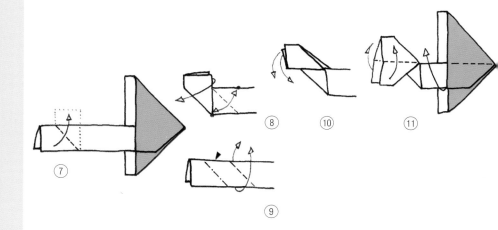

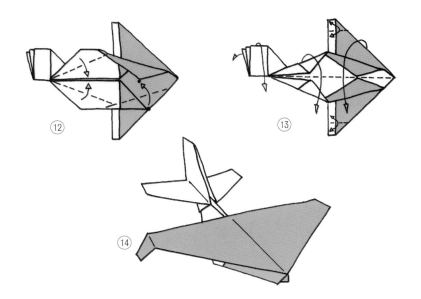

Rafale

This vintage plane is shown in half variants, with different cockpits. This model is a great decoration for an amateur pilot's universe.

For recommended paper, see pp. 137 and139

1 **Fold** the paper in half

2 **Fold in** the right side and left side to the centre, then fold half of the left side out again.

3 **Fold** the right side out, then turn over, unfold half way and turn over

4 **Fold** the sides to the centre fold. Make a valley fold (see p. 10) to force the tips outwards, then fold the tips outwards

5 **Check** your model is as shown, then unfold

6 **Fold** one layer along the fold lines shown (**1**). Fold a layer upwards along the valley fold (see p. 10) (**2**). Fold down the sides of the layer, keeping in the centre

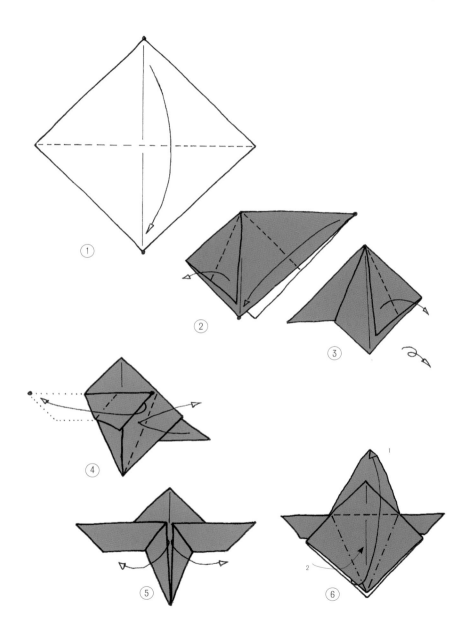

7 **Check** your model is as shown, then turn over

8 **Fold** the tip back on itself at the centre, under the central layer. Fold the two layers to the central layer, then fold the plane in half

9 **Straighten** the wings and flatten the end. Make an inside inverted fold (see p. 11) on the front end

Details

9a **Fold** the front tip towards the back and then wrap from the front, slotting it inside

9b **Open** the tail end out wide

9c **Fold out** the sides of the tail

10 **The** Rafale is ready to take off

Vary the cockpit shape if you choose to

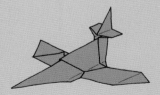

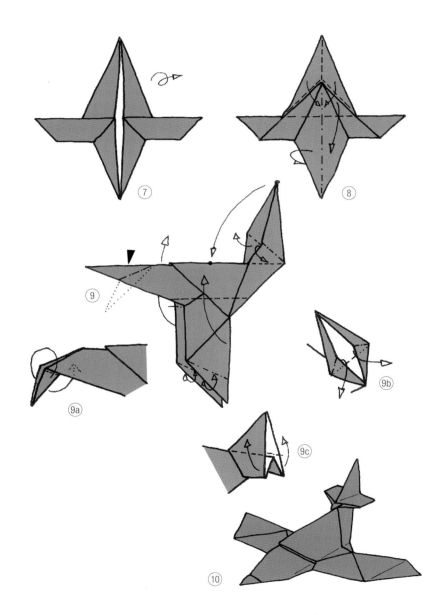

Starship voyager

Get ready for a flight across the universe with this science-fiction film classic.

For recommended paper, see pp. 141 and 143

ready for take off > **30**

1. **Make** a preliminary base (see p. 12) then a bird base (see p. 13). On each side, lift the largest tip towards the top

2. **Fold** the sides of each face

3. **Fold up** each side along the horizontal, then make an inverted fold (see p. 11) on each tip

4. **Fold** the right tip, then bring the central part vertical, folding as shown

   Details for wing tips

4a. **Fold** the tip

4b. **Open** the end

4c. **Refold** the tip of the triangle to the centre, then fold in half

5. **At the base**, fold the triangles both ways, then cut the tip as shown to form the ailerons

6. **Prepare** to fly the finished spaceship

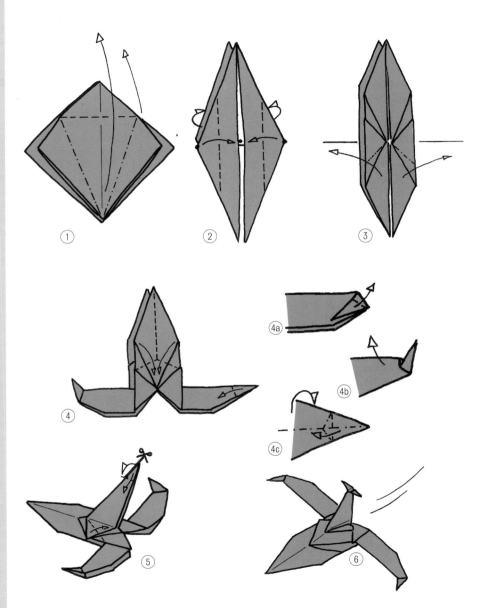

starship voyager > 31

Supersonic jet

The sleek lines of this classic-styled aircraft appear with ease from the magically proportioned rectangle of paper.

For recommended paper, see pp. 145 and 147
Cut to a rectangle measuring 14 x 19.5cm (5½ x 7⅝in)

ready for take off > **32**

1. **Fold** the sides to the centre fold, then turn over

2. **Fold** the sides, leaving the back free

3. **Fold** as shown, then turn over

4. **Fold** to join the dots

5. **Fold** the sides behind

6. **Fold** the tip, as shown

7. **Divide** each side of the tip to the centre, folding the right tab into the back pouch of the tip; then fold the wings along the axis of the plane

8. **Fold** the loose side of the tip to the opposite side, and lock in place with the base of the wing. Fold the wings, joining the two dots along the plane's axis

9. **Fold out** the wings. Make an inverted fold (see p. 11) on the nose of the plane

The plane is complete

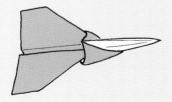

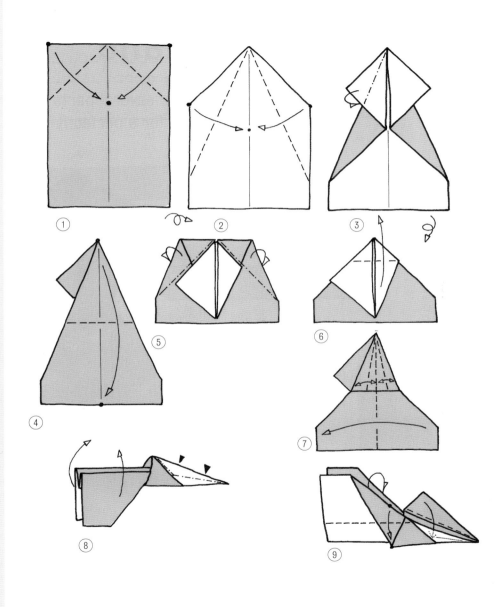

To make the central piece

7a **Fold** the edges of the 14cm (5½in) square as shown and then turn over

7b **Fold** the sides to the centre, keeping the back free, then fold in half along the centre fold

7c **Fold** down the back and then slot in the fuselage and wings from step 6

8 **To hold**, fold the tabs into the central compartment. A cockpit can be added by slotting in a 3 x 6cm (1⅛ x 2⅜in) sheet of paper folded in half as shown

The finished fighter aircraft with cockpit, below, and without cockpit, below right

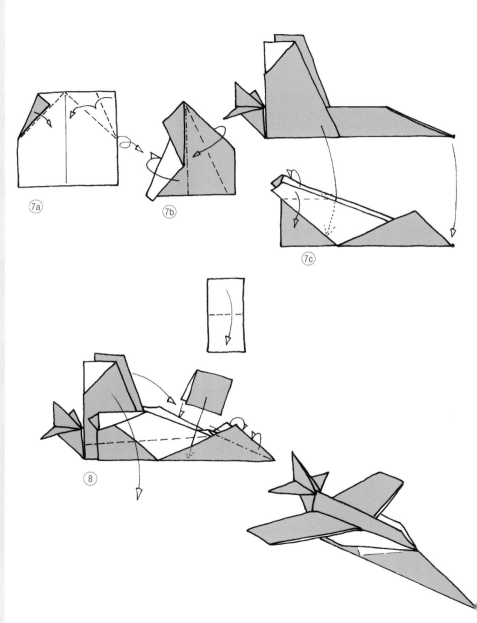

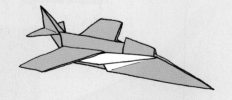

Mirage

The elegant delta-winged Mirage is the classic French fighter jet. This model flies very well if you weigh down the front part.

For recommended paper, see pp. 157 and 159

1 **Fold** the sides into the centre fold

2 **Fold** the tip back to join the dots

3 **Fold** in the sides

4 **Check** your model is as shown, then turn over

5 **Fold** the tip, opening up one side. Then fold the side

6 **Fold** the plane in half

7 **Make** an inside inverted fold (see p. 11) at the rear as indicated by the dotted line

8 **Lift** out the wings and make an inside inverted fold (see p. 11) to form the tail. At the front, fold between the layer to lock the whole thing together

9 **Make** any final adjustments to the Mirage

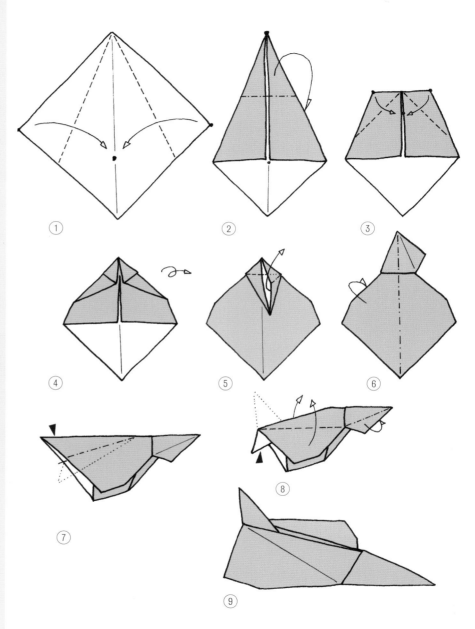

Classic jet

This plane is another fine example of a supersonic aircraft. It will take to the skies if you add a paper clip to the tip.

see pp. 161 and 163

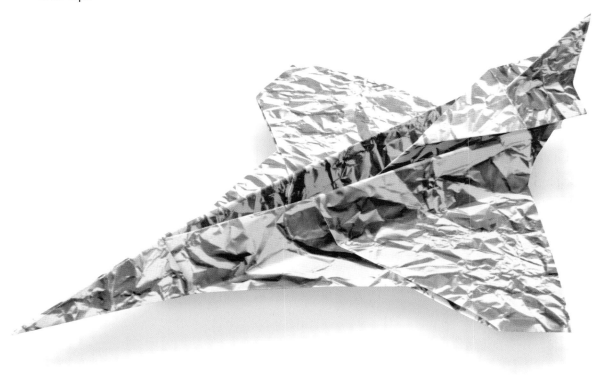

1 **Mark** the creases by folding the sides into the centre as shown

2 **Fold** the tip

3 **Fold** the left side of the tip in half

3a **Fold** the other side of the tip, then fold the sides behind as shown in step 3

4 **Check** your model is as shown, then turn over

5 **Join** the dots

6 **Fold** the tip, then unfold everything

7 **Make** inside inverted folds (see p. 11) as shown

8 **Fold** in half

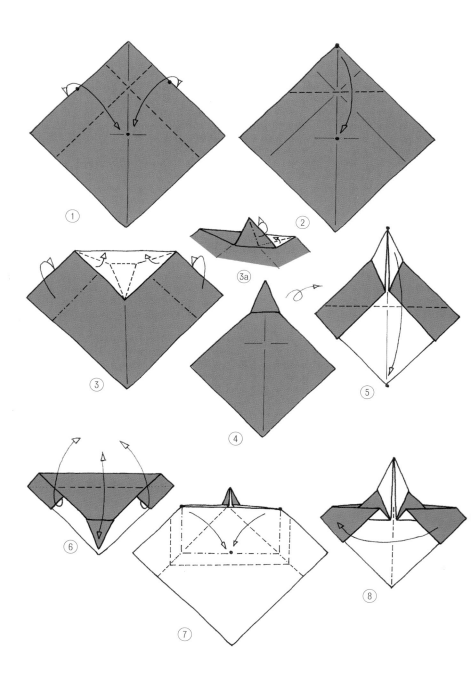

9 **Make** a pre-fold along the dotted line and then make an outside inverted fold (see p. 11)

10 **Fold** out the wings

11 **Make** an outside inverted fold (see p. 11) in the centre, then turn the whole thing over

Details for tail wing

12a **Partially** fold in half

12b **Fold** left side down

12c **Unfold** the triangle

13 **To form the tail**, press the centre to make the central triangle and the ailerons on both sides

Make the final adjustments before launching

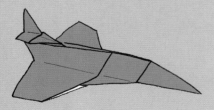

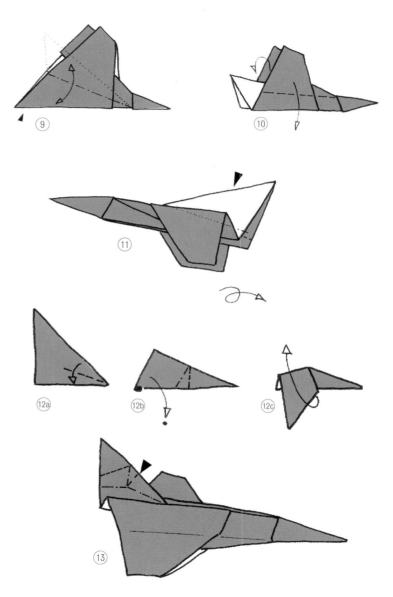

MiG

Here is a plane that flies well indoors and is very easy to make. Each time you launch it, make sure the wings are in a good horizontal position.

For recommended paper, see pp. 165 and 167

1 **Fold** the sides into the centre

2 **Join** the dots

3 **Fold** the tip up, as shown

4 **Fold** the tip as shown

5 **Fold** in the sides

6 **Fold** the plane in two, backwards

7 **Make** an inside inverted fold (see p. 11)

8 **Fold** the wings horizontally at each side

9 **Hold** the plane from underneath to launch it

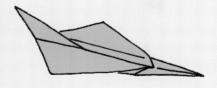

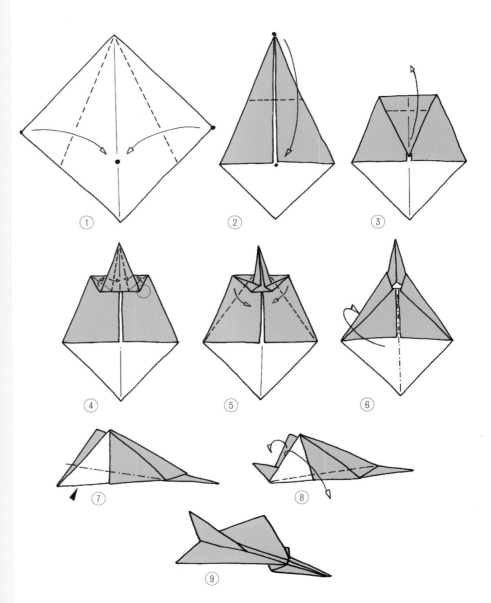

Kit yourself out

Tribal mask

The horns on this ceremonial tribal mask are a symbol of strength.

For recommended paper, see pp. 169 and 171

1 **Make** a bird base (see p. 13). Fold up the tip of the top layer, then fold up the two tips from underneath along the dotted lines, making an outside inverted fold (see p. 11)

2 **Fold** the base of the central tip up and under

3 **Fold** the central tip up and slot under as shown, then fold the two top tips into the centre. Fold the left tip in half as shown

4 **Fold** the right tip to match the left tip, then unfold both tips. At the base of the mask, open the sides, folding upwards

5 **To finish** the mask, fold the central triangle of the two top tips backwards twowards the dots and then push the edges into their folds. Fold down the lower part to form the mouth

6 **Shape** the bottom lip by folding it, then bend the eyebrow arches and push the nose into shape

7 **The tribal mask** is complete

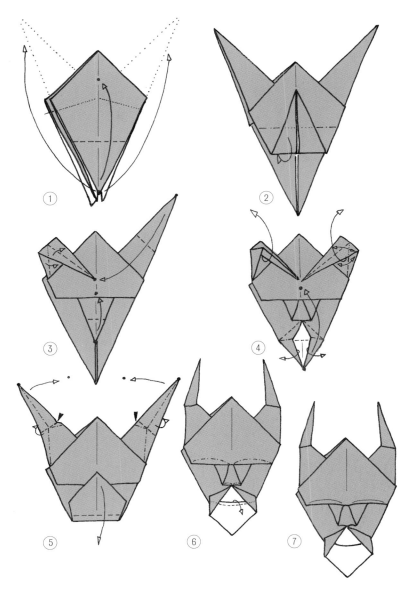

Monkey mask

An animal-print paper is the perfect choice for this monkey mask with its almost human expression.

For recommended paper, see pp. 173 and 175

kit yourself out > **48**

1 **Fold** the tip down and then mark the centre line of the paper by folding in half

2 **Mark** the lower tip and then bend the small central triangle on the top tip without pressing down

3 **Partially fold** the top as shown, holding the mask in your hands to help shape it

4 **Fold** down the upper triangle and then fold in half, opening the sides

To form the eyes, press the tips from behind. To form the ears, make the folds as shown and follow the details in steps 5a and 5b. To form the mouth and give it shape, make a fold on the bottom part and follow the details in step 5c

Details

5a **Fold** the left ear as shown

5b **Fold** the right ear as shown

5c **Fold** the tip down towards the back and then, to form the mouth, fold the centre

6 **The monkey mask** is complete

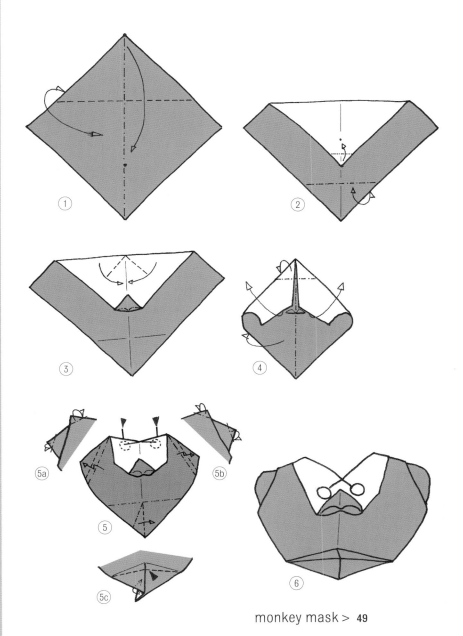

Desert turban

In hot desert landscapes, people protect themselves from the sun and the sun by wrapping several metres of fabric around the head.

For recommended paper,
see pp. 177 and 179

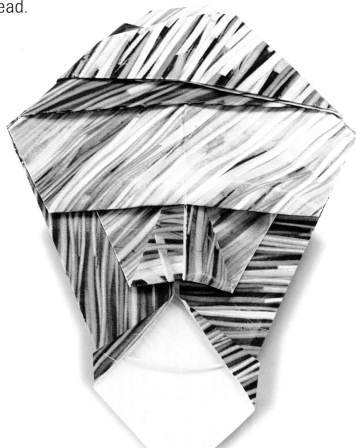

1. **Make** a bird base (see p. 13). Fold up the tip of the top layer towards the top, then fold up the two tips from underneath along the dotted lines using an outside inverted fold (see p. 11)

2. **Fold** the base of the central tip up and under

3. **Fold** the centre triangle under, then fold the tips and tuck the ends inside

4. **Fold** the tip of the turban to the back. To form the mouth, open the sides and fold towards the top. Bend the eyebrow arches and the nose

5. **Fold** the centre triangle, then fold down to form the moustache

6. **The desert turban** is complete

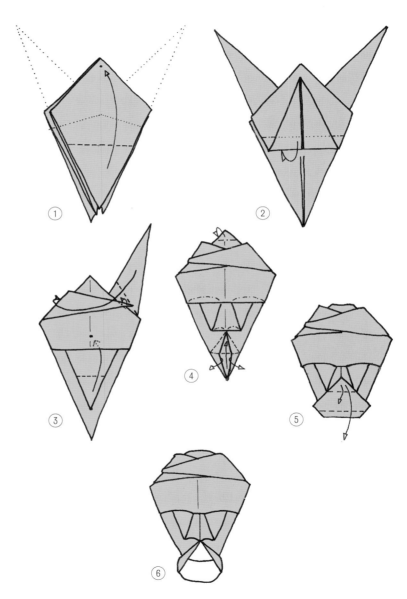

desert turban > 51

Leopard mask

In many tribal ceremonies, it is common to wear masks to symbolically endow the wearer with special powers, like the strength of a leopard for example.

For recommended paper, see pp. 181 and 183

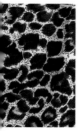

1 **Fold** in half

2 **Fold** the sides down into the centre, as shown

3 **Fold up** the tips, as shown

4 **Unfold**

5 **Open up**, then push flat

6 **Fold** along the fold lines as shown, then repeat on the other side

7 **Fold** one flap to the centre, as shown here with the left-hand side, then fold a triangle, as shown again on the left. Repeat on the right, then turn over

8 **Pinch** the bottom tip, folding it to give it shape

9 **Pinch** the nose, folding the first tip under. Fold back the other tip along the fold lines, then push in the eyebrow arches

10 **The leopard mask** is complete

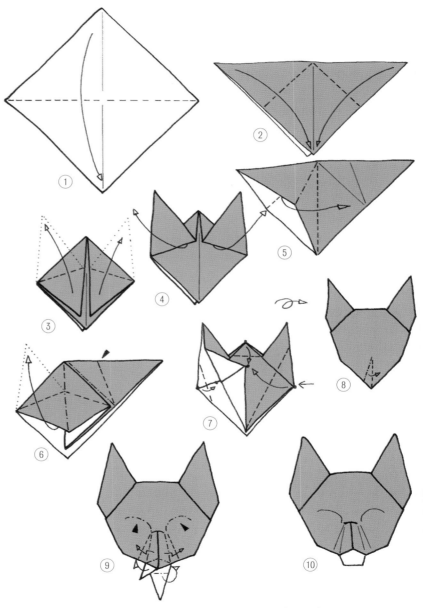

leopard mask > 53

Funny face mask

A pointed nose or a round nose? Blue eyes or black? Open mouth or closed? How your funny face mask turns out is completely up to you.

For recommended paper, see pp. 185 and 187

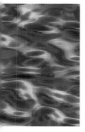

1 **Fold** in half from top to bottom

2 **Fold** the left corner a quarter of the way
  in (**1**), then fold the paper in half from
  side to side (**2**)

3 **Fold** the right corner in as before (**1**),
  then open the origami out (**2**)

4 **Fold** the paper in half, backwards

5 **Fold** the left corner a third of the way
  in, joining the dots

6 **Fold** the right corner in the same way

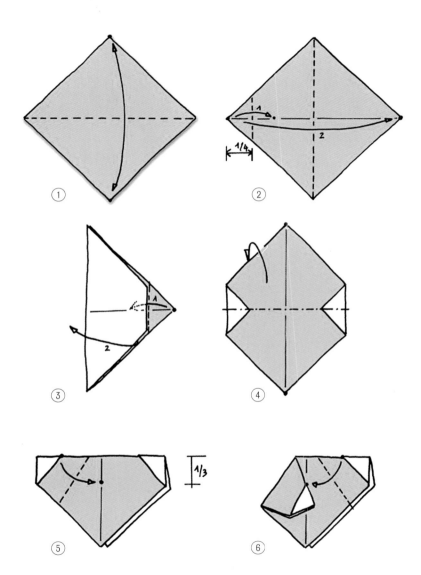

7 **Fold up** the right side, as shown

8 **Fold up** the left side, then turn the whole thing over

9 **Fold** the sides using two valley folds (see p. 10) to match the shape of the reverse side, then press the whole thing flat

10 **To form the nose**, mark the fold along the flap (**1**), then open in half and press flat (**2**)

11 **Make** a fold at either side to form the ears. For the mouth, fold up the top layer only at the tip to the dot, then fold again

12 **To finish the mouth**, fold the back layer of the tip backwards. Give shape to the eyes by folding forwards as shown

13 **Fold** down the part above the eyes to complete the mask

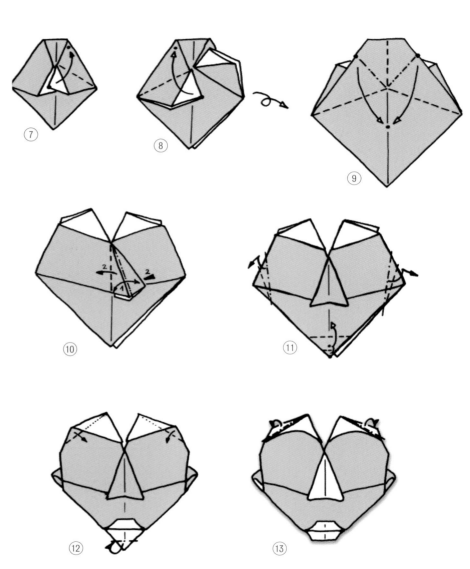

Bow tie

Made from fancy coloured paper of your choosing, this bow tie is the last word in geek chic.

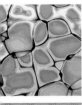

For recommended paper, see pp. 189, 190, 191, 193 and 195
Cut a strip 3cm (1½in) wide as marked on reverse

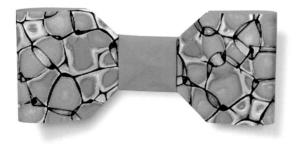
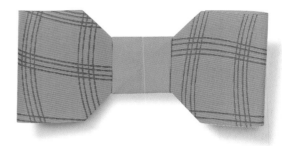

1. **Cut** a strip as marked on the reverse of the paper

2. **Fold** the paper strip in half

3. **Fold in** the corners of the folded edge to meet, then unfold

4. **Fold** an inside inverted fold (see p. 11) at each corner

5. **Fold up** the strip at back and front as shown

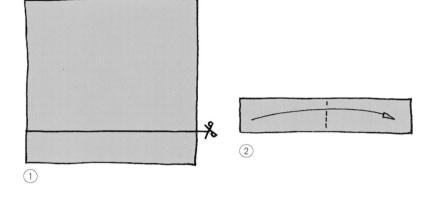

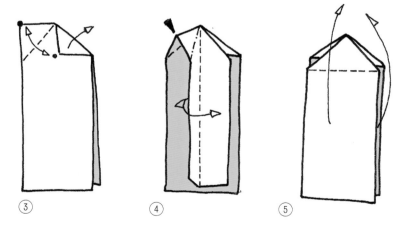

6   **Fold** the corners of each side once again

7   **Hold** the folded corners with both hands, close together, then pull outwards to form the central square

8   **Check** your model is as shown

9   **Mark** the folds of the four corners at the ends

10 **Unfold** the central section to curve in the ends. Lock it all in place, folding the central part into the folds

The bow tie is complete

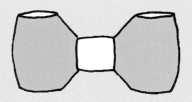

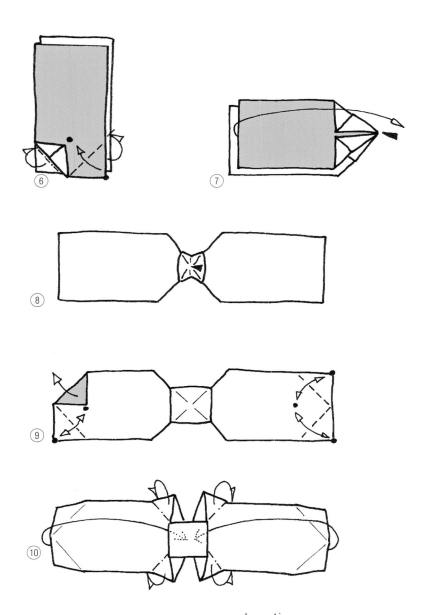

Tie

Make a trendy little tie to suit your individual style from the choice of patterned papers provided.

For recommended paper, see pp. 197, 199 and 201

1 **Fold** the tip to join the dots

2 **Fold up** the tip and then turn over

3 **Fold** the sides into the centre

4 **Fold outwards**, as shown, then fold the left side into the centre. Unfold the triangles from under the folds

5 **Fold** the right side and then fold the upper left triangle in half

6 **Fold** the right side to match

7 **Cross** the sides symmetrically to the centre, fold down the tip of the triangle at the very top, then turn the whole thing over

The tie is complete

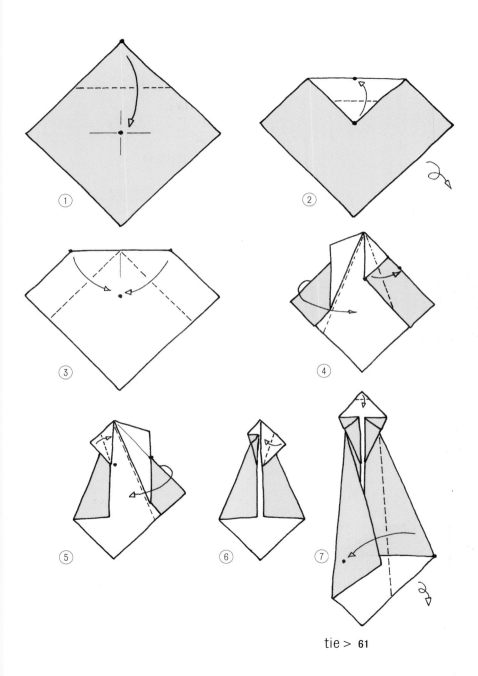

Kimono

Stay zen by making a classic kimono from Japanese print papers.

For recommended paper, see pp. 203, 205 and 207
Cut in half as marked on reverse

kit yourself out > **62**

1 **Fold back** the top edge of a half square

2 **Fold** the corners to the centre fold

3 **Check** your model is as shown, then turn over

4 **Fold up** along the horizontal

5 **Fold** the back edge down, joining the dots, then unfold the central part

6 **Fold** the central part back up to join the dots, then fold the top folded edge behind

7 **Fold** the sides to the centre, as shown

8 **Open** the sides, as shown on the left side, then fold the central part back down

9 **To form the sleeves**, fold the top part behind and fold up the bottom flaps as shown

10 **The kimono** is complete

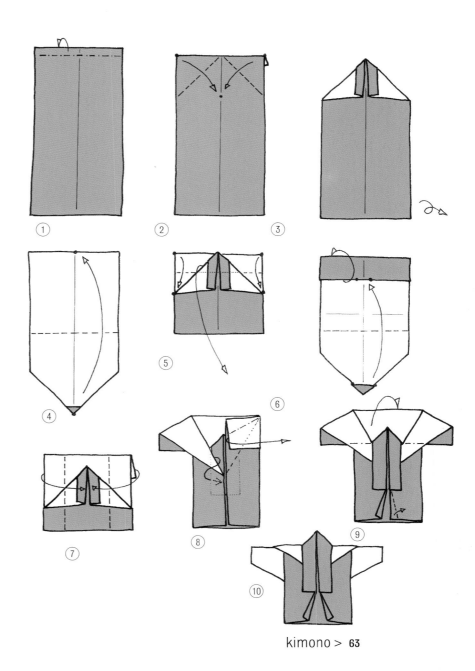

kimono > **63**

Glasses

This fun pair of glasses will help you to see life in multicolour

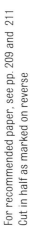

For recommended paper, see pp. 209 and 211
Cut in half as marked on reverse

1 **Fold** the half square to join the dots as shown

2 **Mark** the centre fold, then unfold completely

3 **Refold** along the diagonal

4 **Mark** the folds half way up, then quarter of the way up

5 **Fold** each half along the folds shown by rolling

6 **To form the glasses**, fold the tips back and then fold the sides round and pinch the centre. Turn the whole thing over

7 **The pair of glasses** is complete

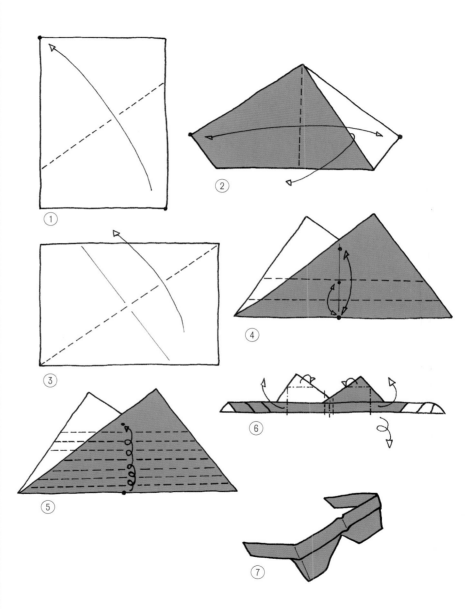

T-shirt

A t-shirt makes a great canvas to express your creativity. Which hand-drawn print will you choose?

For recommended paper, see pp. 213, 215 and 217
Cut in half as marked on reverse

1 **Cut** a half-square

2 **Fold** the sides in leaving a gap in the centre

3 **Fold back** a strip at the top for the collar

4 **Fold** the top corners to the centre level with the strip; then mark the fold on the lower edge

5 **Before folding** the lower edge, open the sides out wide

6 **Make** an inside inverted fold (see p. 11) on each side on the folded lower edge, then fold up to the collar to join the dots

7 **The t-shirt** is complete

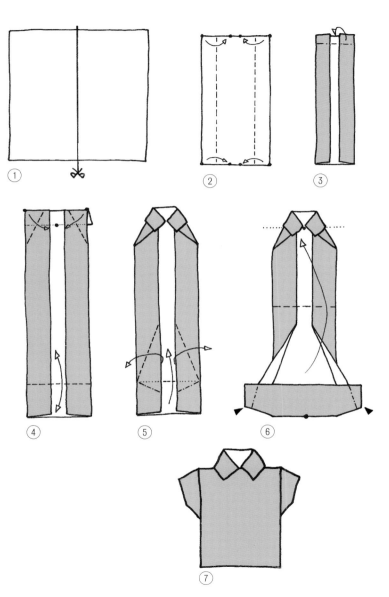

Moroccan slippers

You will require two sheets of paper to make each pair of these classic Moroccan slippers or babouches.

For recommended paper, see pp. 219, 221, 223 and 225

1 **Fold** the paper in half

2 **Fold** in half on all sides. Then unfold and refold the bottom corners to the centre

3 **Check** your model is as shown, then turn over

4 **Fold** the sides as shown. Fold one layer to the inside as shown here on the left side

5 **Slot** the central part inside

6 **Cross over** the two tips

7 **To finish** slide the tips into the folds

8 **The slipper** is complete. Make another for a pair

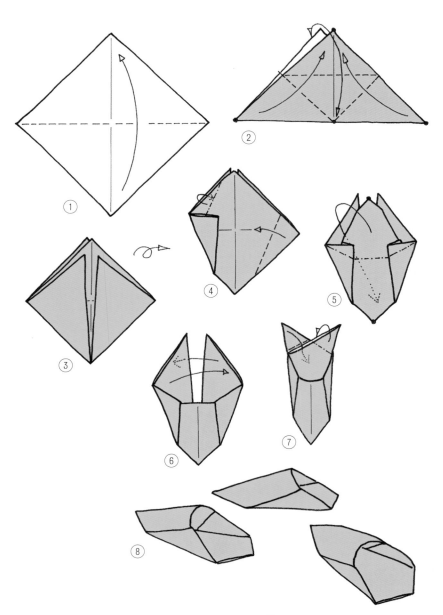

morrocan slippers > **69**

Wallet

Making a wallet from just one sheet of paper is a practical solution for safely storing your business cards, cinema tickets and stamps.

For recommended paper, see pp. 227 and 229

1   **Fold back** a 3.5cm (1⅜in) strip along
    the top edge of the paper square

2   **Fold in** 1cm (⅜in) at each side

3   **Fold up** a 2.5cm (1in) strip at the
    bottom edge

4   **Fold** the top edge to join the dotsinside
    the lower part. Fold the edges of the
    lower part under the top folded part

5   **Mark** two folds in the centre

6   **The wallet** is ready to be filled

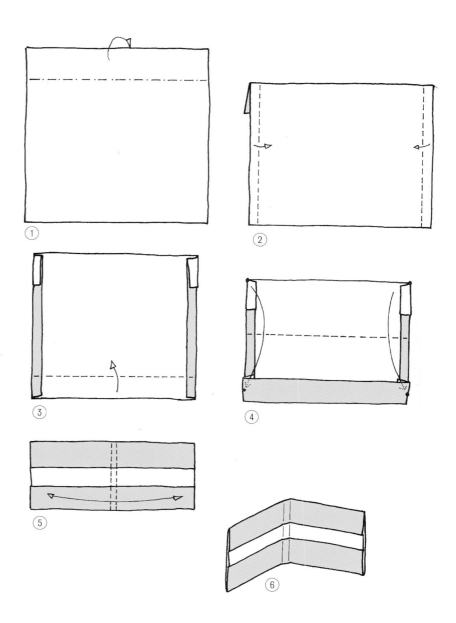

All at sea

Speedboat

Water-bubble printed paper is perfect for modelling this small speedboat as a reminder of holidays by the sea.

For recommended paper, see pp. 231 and 233

1 **Mark** the diagonals

2 **Fold** the corners to the centre and then unfold three of them

3 **Fold over** the tips of the three unfolded corners and then refold

4 **Check** your model is as shown, then turn over

5 **Fold in** the sides to the centre

6 **Turn** one flap to the right

7 **Fold** the top corner and then mark the bottom corner

8 **Lift** one layer. Fold the right tip back

9 **Fold** the sides as shown

10 **Fold** the flap over to the left

11 **Turn** the second layer to the left

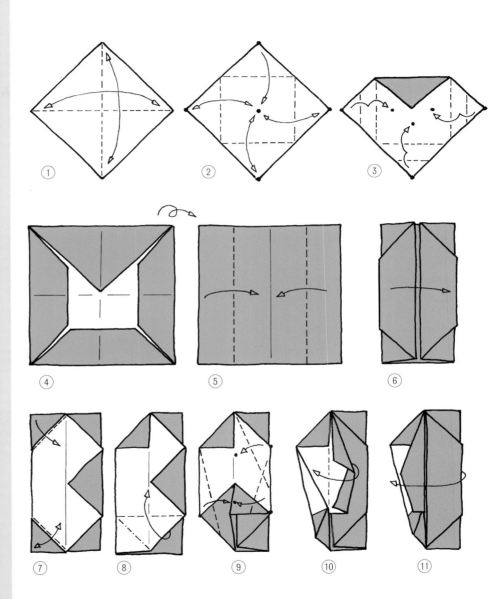

12 Fold the top corner, then fold up one layer at the base

13 Fold the sides as shown

14 Fold the flap over to the right

15 Refold the top triangles as shown

16 Open with both hands, turning the whole inside out like a sock

17 Lift the flap

Detail

17a To form the windshield, fold as shown

18 Flatten the front by folding in each side

The speedboat is complete

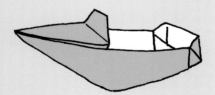

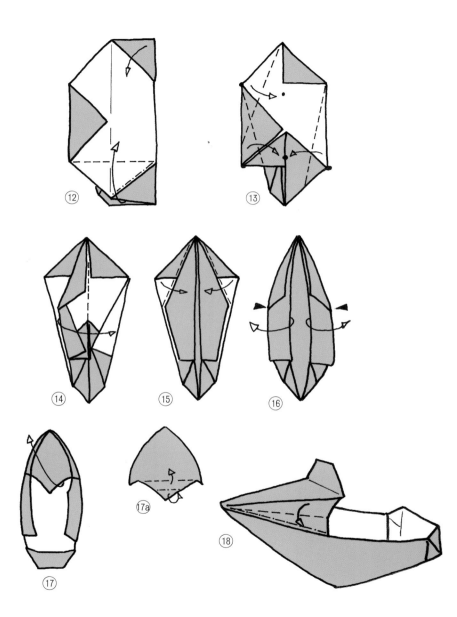

Seabird

Capture the seabirds' flight as they follow the fishermen's boats in search of a fresh fish snack.

For recommended paper, see pp. 235 and 237
Cut in half diagonally as marked on reverse

1. **Mark** the half and quarter points on the left side of your half square as shown. Fold the left side over the centre, joining the dots as shown

2. **Fold back** over to the left. Fold the right side in the same way as the left

3. **Check** your model is as shown, then turn over

4. **Fold** the sides into the centre

5. **Pull** the two tips and turn over

6. **Make** a fold on each side as shown

7. **Fold down** the top to join the dots

8. **Holding** the central part, stretch out the tips and then push flat

9. **Fold** the tip up, as shown

10. **Sharpen** the tip by folding as shown

11. **Fold** the central triangle before folding the whole thing in half

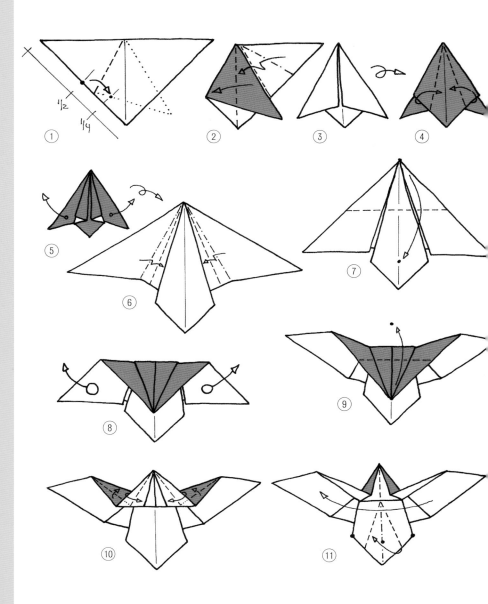

12 **At the rear**, fold the bottom of each side. At the front, make an inside inverted fold (see p. 11)

13 **To form the beak** make two outside inverted folds (see p. 11) on the front. To shape the wings, make a series of folds as shown

Details

13a **To finish**, open the sides

13b **And release** the head

14 **The bird** is ready to fly

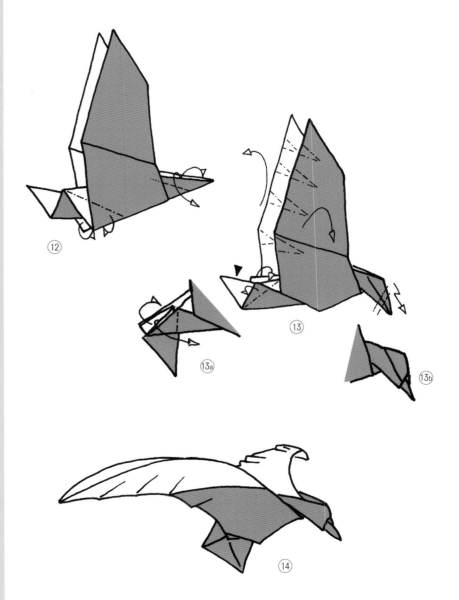

(12)

(13)

(13a)

(13b)

(14)

Nautilus

The nautilus is a living organism with a spiral-shaped shell that looks like it grows outwards from a central point.

For recommended paper, see pp. 239 and 241

1 **Fold** two corners to the centre

2 **Fold** to join the dots

3 **Fold** the bottom edge up, then turn over

4 **Fold** the triangle as shown

5 **Fold** the triangle between the layers,
   then fold the right side, joining the dots

6 **Fold** as shown to join the dots

7 **Fold** as shown to join the dots

8 **Fold** again

9 **Fold** into the centre

10 **Fold** one last time, then slide inside

11 **The nautilus** is complete

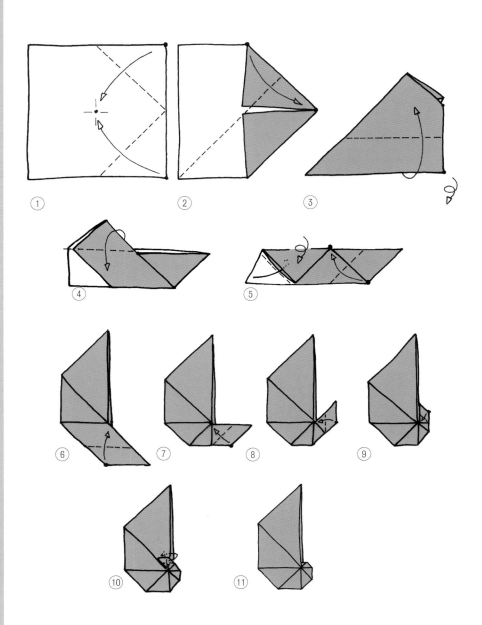

Windsurfing board

Windsurfing is a cross between sailing and surfing but you won't get very far without your very own windsurfing board.

For recommended paper, see pp. 243 and 245

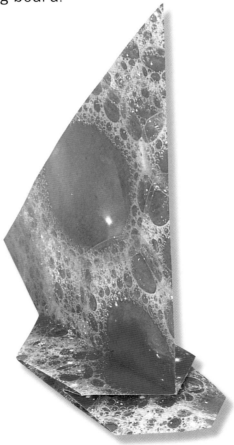

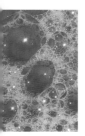

1 **Fold** in half

2 **Join** the dots

3 **Open** and then flatten

4 **Fold** the top and bottom edges to form triangles

5 **Fold** the triangles in half, then unfold

6 **Make** inside inverted folds (see p. 11) with the two triangles

7 **Fold** to the left to reveal the inside and then fold horizontally

8 **Fold** the ends

9 **The windsurfing board** is complete

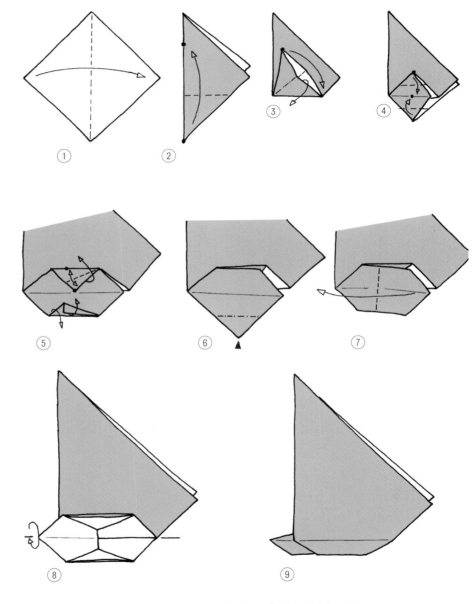

windsurfing board > **83**

Sailboat

A printed paper that captures the effect of light rippling on water is the perfect choice for this model of a sailboat.

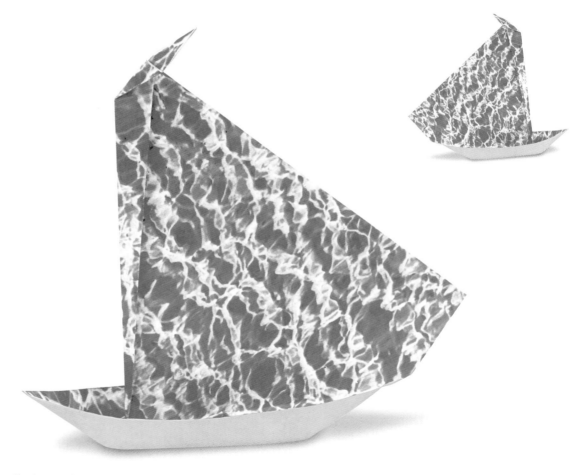

For recommended paper, see pp. 247 and 249

1 **Follow** steps 1 to 4 of the windsurfing board (see p. 83), this time folding the triangles on the diagonal

2 **Open up** the triangle at the base to give you a large diamond shape. To form the mast, fold a thin strip of the paper along the folded edge as shown

3 **Fold** the top and bottom tips of the diamond to the dot in the centre

4 **To form the hull**, open widely and turn inside out like a sock. Finally, fold the top of the mast to make the flag

The sailboat is complete

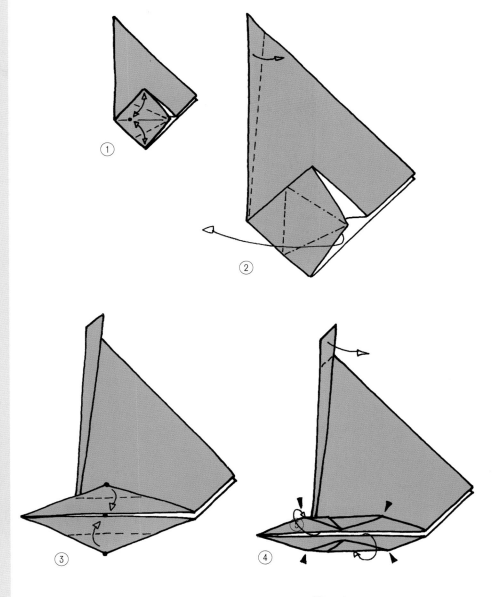

①

②

③

④

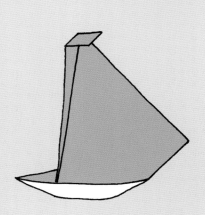

Canoe

This lightweight boat allows you to be at one with nature, navigating rivers and streams, and moving with skill to avoid taking in water.

For recommended paper, see pp. 251 and 253

1 **Fold** the side corners to the centre

2 **Fold** each triangle as shown

3 **Fold** each side as shown on the right. Check your folded triangles match the one on the left, then turn over

4 **Fold** the sides into the centre

5 **Fold** the ends over at the top and bottom, then fold the top triangle in half sliding it between the layers; then slide the tips one inside the other in the centre

6 **Finally,** fold the other end in half, sliding it between the layers

7 **The canoe** is complete

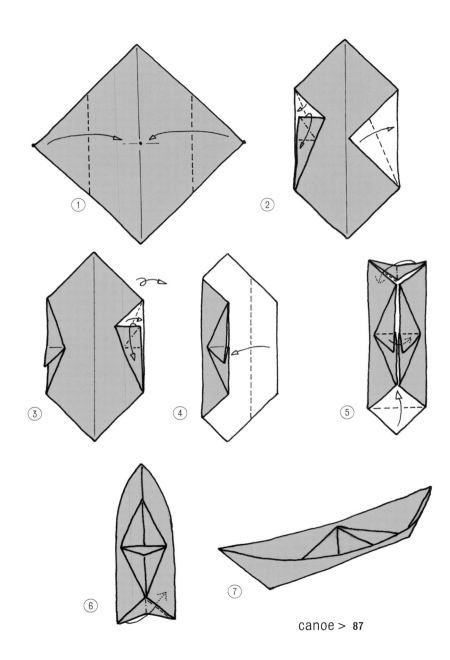

Fish

A paper printed with large water bubbles is the perfect choice for making this little fish. Why not make a shoal?

For recommended paper, see pp. 255 and 257

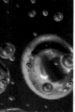

1 **Fold** the sides to the centre

2 **Fold up** the bottom triangle, slotting it under the side flaps

3 **Fold back** the bottom edges of the side flaps as shown

4 **Unfold** the bottom triangle, then turn over

5 **Fold down** the top, joining the dots

6 **Fold in** the sides, opening the triangles at the bottom

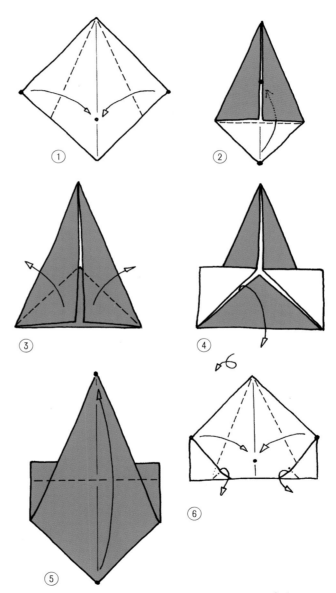

7 **Fold** the bottom triangle in the centre, then slide it between the layers before folding the whole thing in half

8 **Fold up** the triangle on the front of the fish, connecting the dots. At the rear, mark the fold along the dotted line

9 **Fold back** the top triangle at the head. To form the tail, make an outside inverted fold (see p. 11) on all layers, then turn over

10 **Fold** the other side of the head and then, to finish the tail, turn the tip up

11 **To finish**, fold the top of the head back between the layers.

12 **The fish** is complete

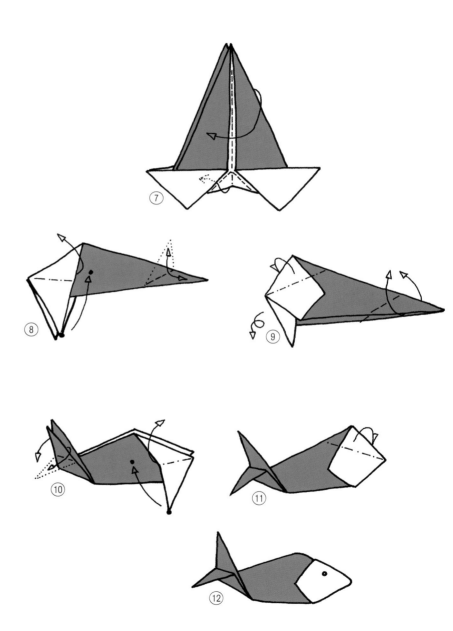

Dolphin

Dolphins move around in pods, having races offshore, so you may want to make a few.

For recommended paper, see pp. 259 and 261

1. **Make** a bird base (see p. 13) then lift up one layer

2. **Fold** the two tips as shown by the dotted line, then fold up. Make a 1.5cm (⅝in) cut on the back part

3. **Make** an inside inverted fold (see p. 11) on each tip, then turn over

4. **Fold** the tips inside. Fold the sides of the central triangle and then fold the whole thing in half vertically

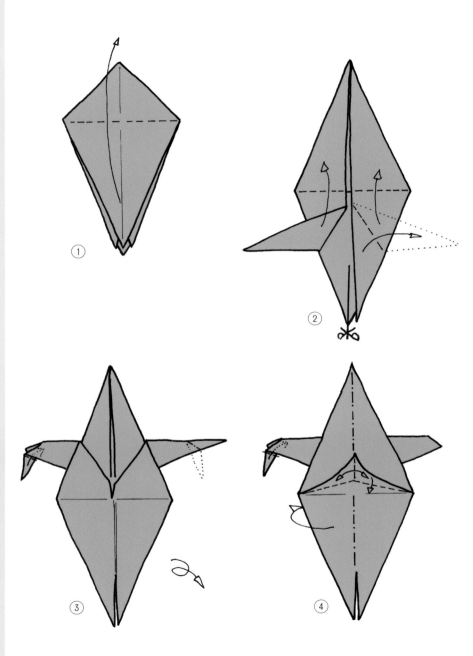

① ② ③ ④

5 **On the left**, fold along the dotted line and then fold the end to form the tail. On the right side, fold the tip back

6 **On the left**, fold upwards and then fully unfold. On the right, fold the tip and then open fully

Details for tail

6a **Make** two inside and outside inverted folds (see p. 11)

6b **Fold under**

Details for head

6c **Make** two inside inverted folds (see p. 11) then fold behind the end

6d **To finish the head**, fold the corners under, then flatten the tip

The dolphin is complete

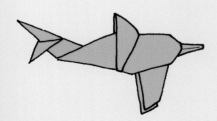

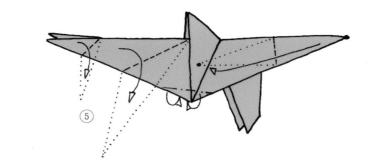

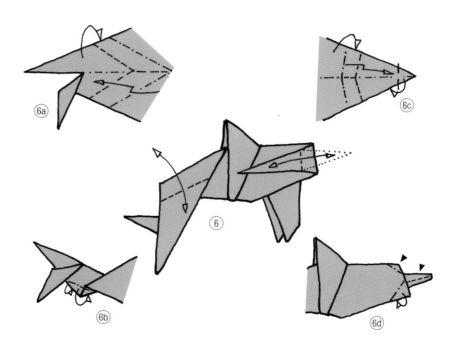

Crab

What better way to spend a day at the beach than rock-pooling for this small seaside crustacean?

For recommended paper, see pp. 263 and 265

1   **Mark** the mid-way point on both sides and then fold the paper in half

2   **Fold** forward and back as shown

3   **Open** wide and then flatten

4   **Check** your model is as shown, then fold the top down to join the dots

5   **To form the claws**, make two inside inverted folds (see p. 11) as shown

6   **To form the front pincers**, make a fold as shown. To form the back claws, bend back. Push into shape, pressing lightly on the centre triangle

7   **The crab** is complete

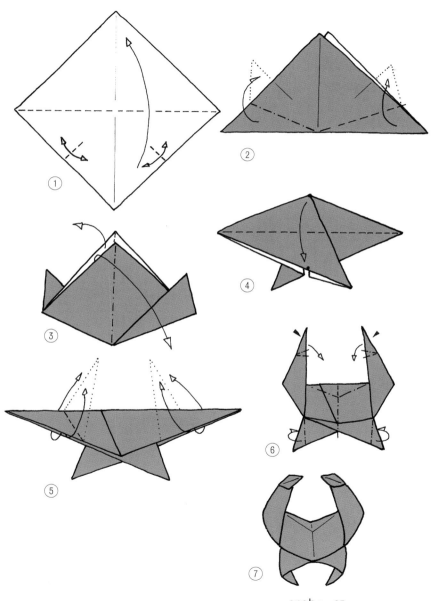

crab > 95

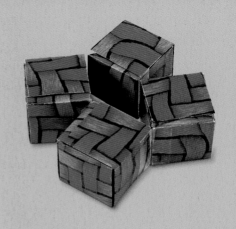

Construction site

Cube

This cube is made from six folded units that slot together. Cut six small squares from one and a half sheets of paper to make it.

For recommended paper, see pp. 267, 269, 271, 273 and 275 Use one and a half sheets and cut into six small squares as marked on reverse

To fold the units

1   **Fold** a small square in thirds (see p. 11). Fold the left corner over to join the dots

2   **Fold back** to join the dots

3   **Repeat** to make a pleat fold on the right side

4   **Fold in** the triangles at the top and bottom

5   **Slide** the top and bottom triangles inside as shown

6   **Mark** the end folds. These triangles are used for tabs during assembly. Make six units in all

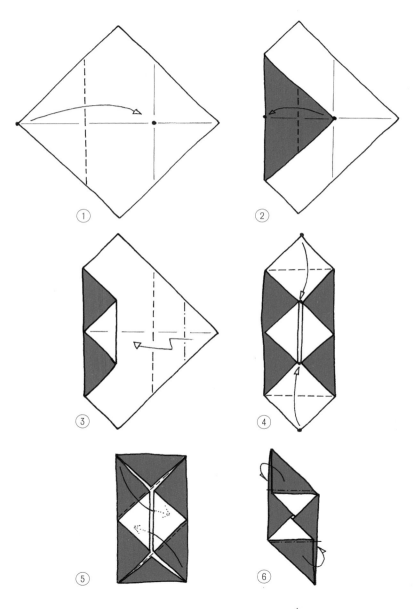

To assemble the units

7 **Slot** the tab of the first piece between the layers of the second

8 **Slot** the tabs of the third piece as before, then turn over

9 **Position** the final three pieces, as before

10 **The cube** is complete

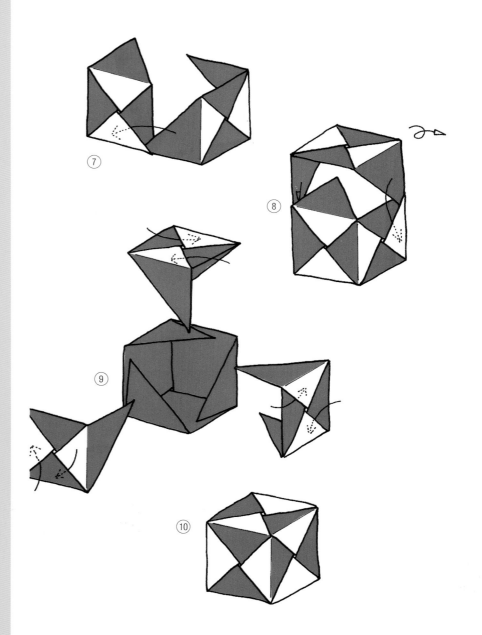

Boulder

The boulder is made from 12 folded units that slot together in a similar way to the cube (see p. 99). You can make other shapes by adding more pieces.

(see p. 99)

Use three sheets cut into 12 small squares as marked on reverse

1 **Make** the cube base (see p. 99) up to
   step 6. Make four units from each sheet.
   On each unit, mark the diagonal of the
   central square, then fold the triangular
   tabs in half

2 **Join** four units, sliding each tab under
   the layer of each square

3 **Add** another unit to the four free tabs,
   then add in the last four pieces to close
   the boulder

4 **The boulder** is complete

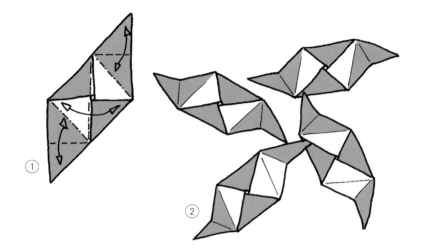

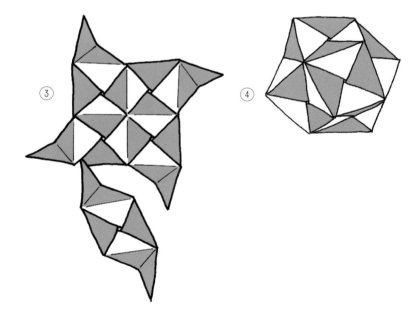

Articulated cubes

Each cube is made from a single sheet of paper. Concealed hinges are used to join the cubes in a group of four, then eight, so that the assembled cubes can change shape.

For recommended paper, see pp. 283, 285, 287, 289, 291, 293 and 295
For each cube, one sheet of paper is required

1 **Fold** the corners of a small square to the centre, then mark the folds in thirds

2 **Open** completely, then turn over

3 **Fold back** the two triangles and mark the last folds as shown, then turn over

4 **Slot** the sides in, one inside the other

5 **Fold** the two triangles at the ends and then lift the sides

6 **To close up**, fit together the two ends

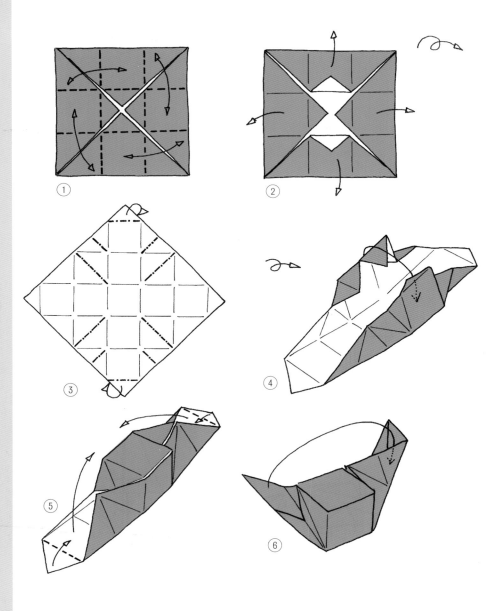

7 **The completed cube**. Make a total of eight cubes in this way

8 **Join together** four cubes with adhesive tape as shown

9 **Push** on opposite sides...

10 **...to articulate** the cubes

11 **Assemble** eight cubes as shown

12 **Cubes connected** in this way can pivot on their hinges

13 **Continue to pivot** your model on its hinges to change its shape

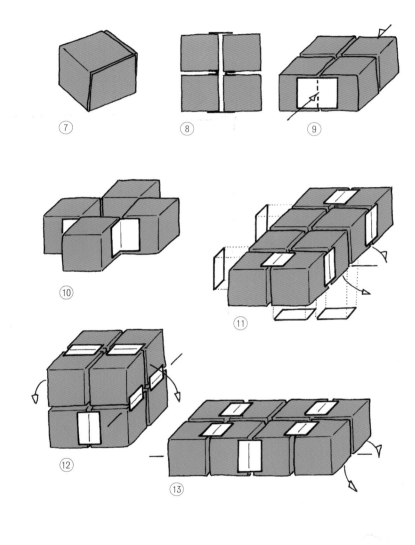

Standing star

At the centre of this star is a cube base. Each of the tips is folded individually, then slotted in place onto the cube.

For recommended paper, see pp. 297, 299, 301 and 303. Use three sheets, cut into 12 small squares as marked on reverse

1 **Make** a cube (see p. 99) and set it aside. Fold a waterbomb base (see p. 12), then fold one side along the centre fold

2 **Mark** the mountain fold (see p. 11) of the lower tip, then turn one flap to the left

3 **Fold** the second face in the same way as the first

4 **Mark** the mountain fold (see p. 11) of the lower tip, then turn the flap to the right

5 **Check** your model is as shown, then turn over

6 **Repeat** for the third face

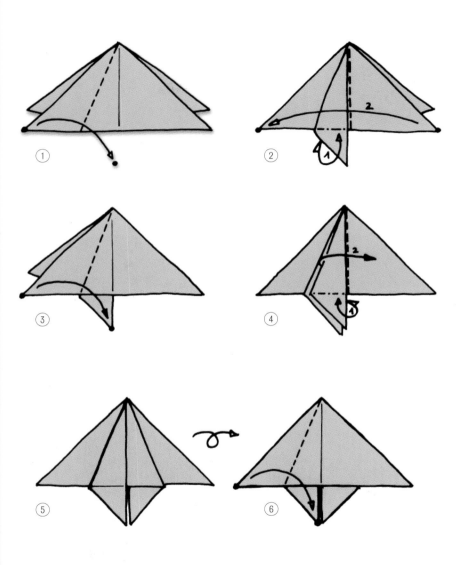

7 **Mark** the fold of the tip and then turn the flap to the left

8 **Repeat** for the final face

9 **Mark** the fold of the tip and then fold the flap to the right

10 **Make** six units in all following steps 1 to 9. Push each of the completed units into shape by folding the four tips at the base of each. You now have the six arms of your star. Slot each tip into the sides of the cube

11 **The star is complete**. To keep everything together, the different parts can be glued

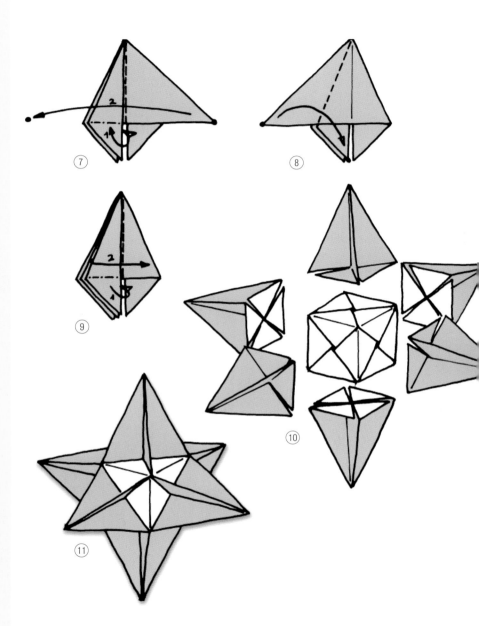

Satellite

This assembled structure could be a satellite tumbling through space, or maybe even a spacecraft. Make 12 bars and six stars, then slot them together for a shape that is out of this world.

Use four and a half sheets of paper. Cut 12 small squares for the bars and six small squares for the tips, as marked on reverse

To make the bars

1 **Mark** the centre fold

2 **Fold** the sides into the centre fold

3 **Fold** the four corners as shown

4 **Unfold** completely

5 **Fold** the top triangles. Make outside inverted folds (see p. 11) by folding the sides

6 **Take** the tips as shown in both hands, then pull outwards

7 **Fold in** the central triangle and then press flat

8 **Repeat** steps 5 to 7 at the bottom edge

9 **Fold** in half as shown

10 **The bar is complete**. Make a total of 12 bars

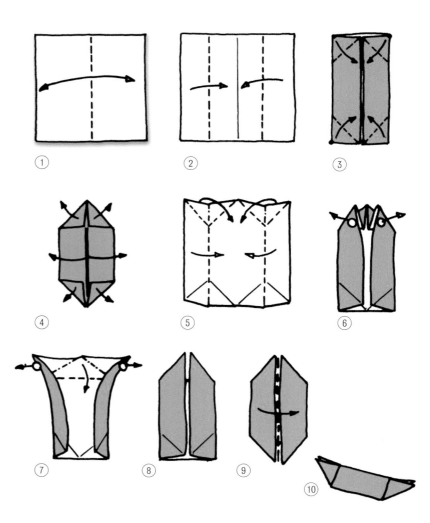

To make the stars

11 **Make** a waterbomb base (see p. 12), then fold the four tips to the top

12 **Fold** the four tips down

13 **Unfold** fully and then press the centre to invert the folds

14 **Fold** along the fold lines into a preliminary base (see p. 12)

15 **Pinch** the tip in half, marking the folds as shown (**1**), then lift the flap (**2**). Repeat for the reverse

16 **Turn** one flap to the right and, on the reverse, one flap to the left, then repeat step 15 for the other two sides

17 **The star is complete**. Make a total of six squares

To assemble the satellite

18 **Slide** each tip of the star between the layers of each bar

19 **For this variation**, omit the stars and angle the bars

20 **For a slightly different look**, lift the tips of the stars

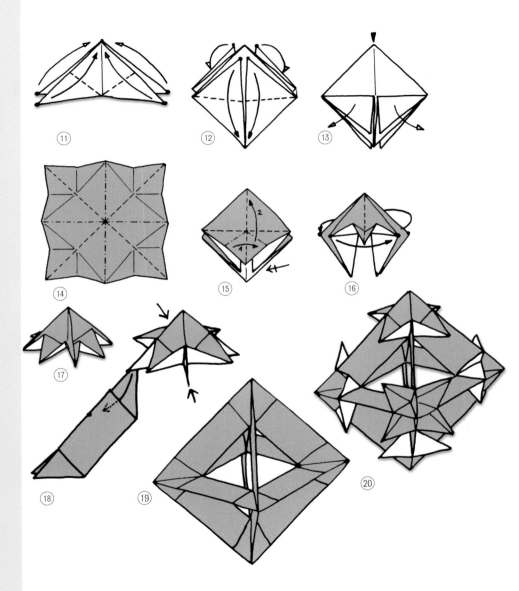

Sphere

This magnificent sphere is made from 20 folded units. It can be suspended from a wire or put on a shelf for an eye-catching decoration. Explore what other forms are possible.

For recommended paper, see pp. 321, 323, 325, 327, 329, 331 and 333
Use four sheets and cut six small triangles from each as marked on reverse

1 **Mark** the folds, folding the sides in half

2 **Fold** the tips to the centre, as shown

3 **Open** the tips out, then join the dots

4 **Fold out** along the marked fold joining the dots

5 **Repeat** for the second tip

6 **Repeat** again for the last tip, sliding it under the first

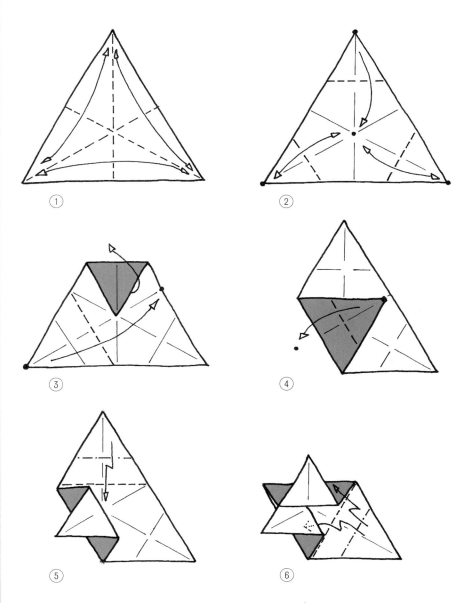

7 **Fold** the triangles, then turn over

8 **Give** the item shape, as shown.

9 **Make** 20 units in total following steps
   1 to 8. Join two units by sliding the tip of
   one between the layers of the other

10 **Join** five units to form a ring.

11 **The sphere** is closed when all the five
    unit rings are complete and joined to
    each other by connecting each free tip
    to another unit

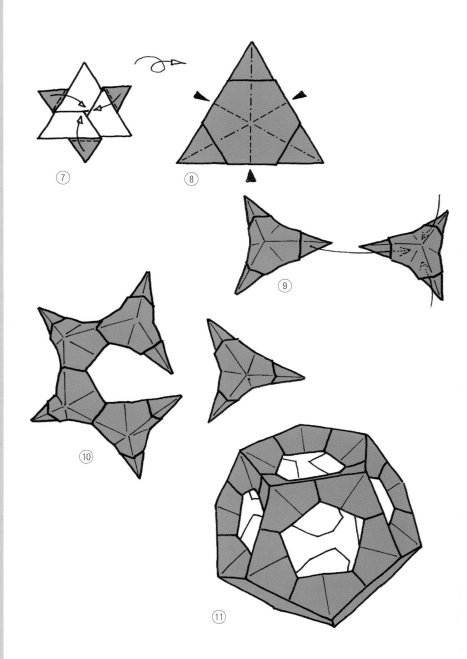

Ninja star

This star is made with two strips of paper folded in a symmetrical manner. Accuracy in your folding is essential for the success of this model.

For recommended paper, see pp. 335, 337 and 339
Cut sheet in half as marked on reverse, then in half again

1 **Fold** a sheet in half, then fold one half in half again, and cut these strips

2 **Fold** the corners of the two strips as shown

3 **Fold** again as shown to make 4a and 4b

4a **Turn** this unit over and continue to fold as shown in step 5a

4b **Fold** the right triangle back to complete the base unit

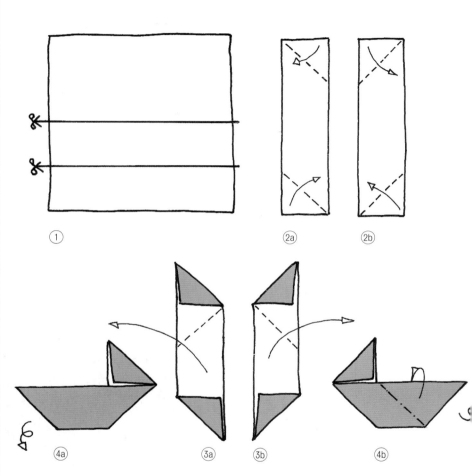

① ②a ②b

④a ③a ③b ④b

5a Return to the second unit and fold the left triangle forward

5b Check your model is as shown

6a Place this unit on the base unit as shown

6b Fold two triangles as shown, slotting the tips into the centre

7 Check your model is as shown, then turn over

8 Fold the other two triangles as before

The star is complete

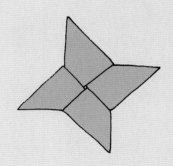

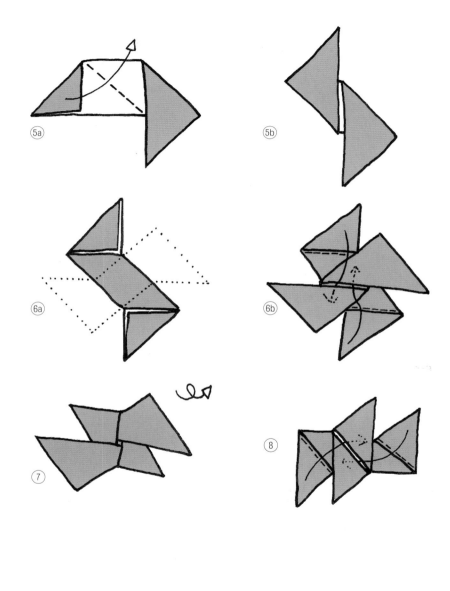

Pliers

A pair of quite useless but nonetheless amazing pliers!
They move by simply squeezing the ends.

1 **Fold** the paper in half

2 **Fold** in half again

3 **Mark** the tip as shown, and open up to the half fold

4 **Mark** the folds as shown, then unfold completely

5 **Fold** the sides together and then fold the whole thing up (see fish base p. 13)

6 **Mark** the folds

7 **Place** each side vertically, then open by pressing the tip to form a triangle

8 **Check** your model is as shown, then turn over

9 **Fold** the sides

10 **Fold** the tips in half, then separate the handles to mark the central diamond inside the jaws

11 **Operate** the pliers by opening or closing the handles

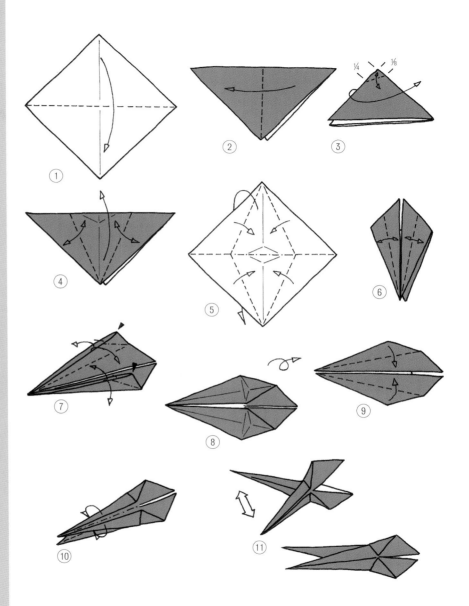

pliers > 119

Paper

On the following pages you will find the various papers that were used to make the origami shown in this book. There are also stickers available so you can let you imagination run wild and add character to your origami model.

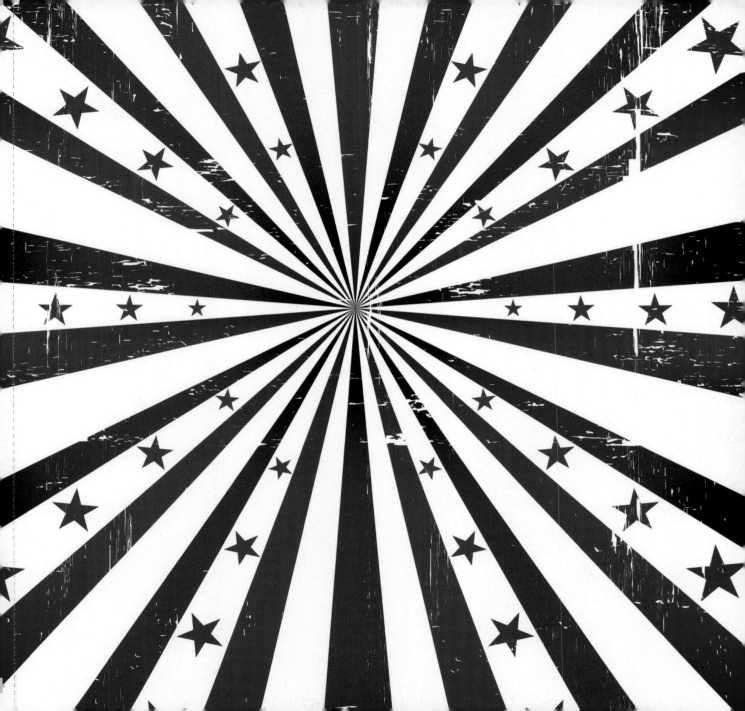

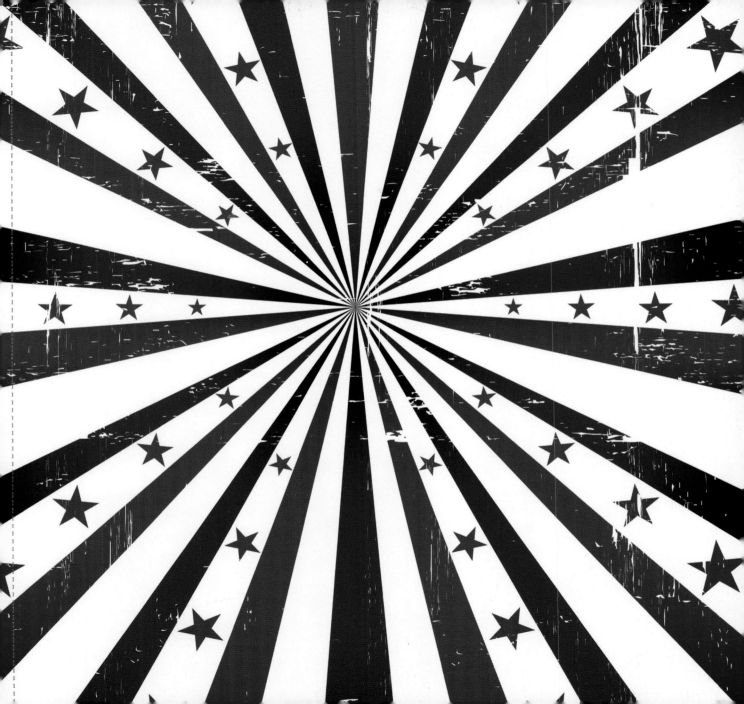

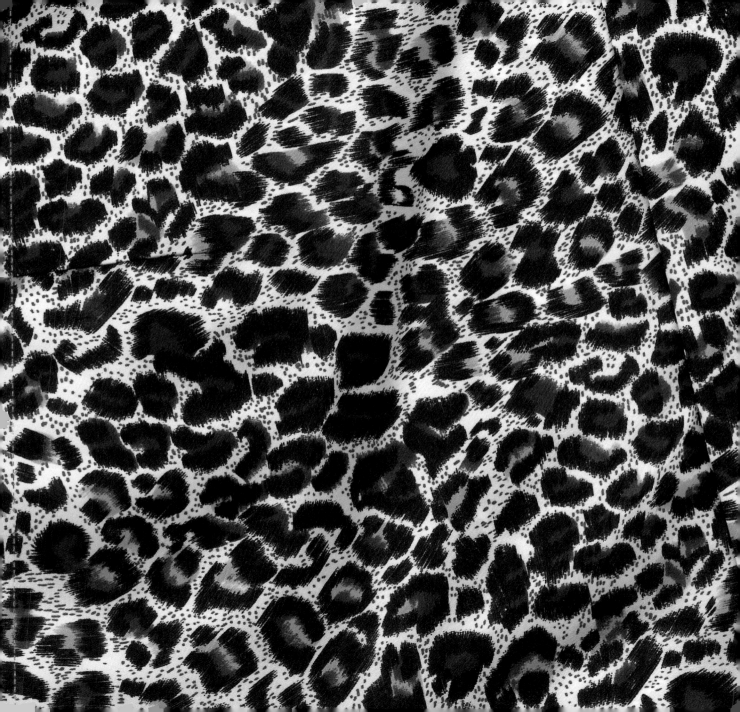

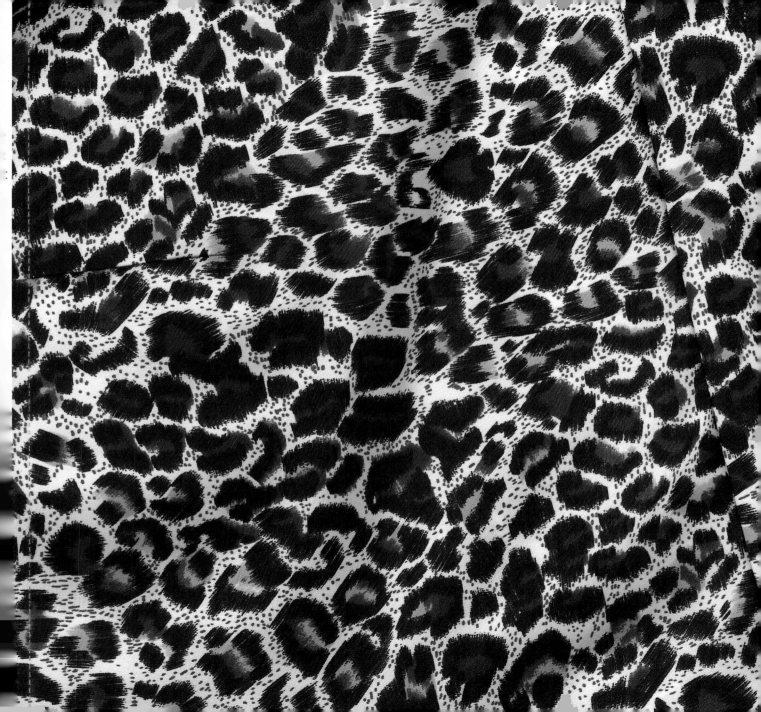

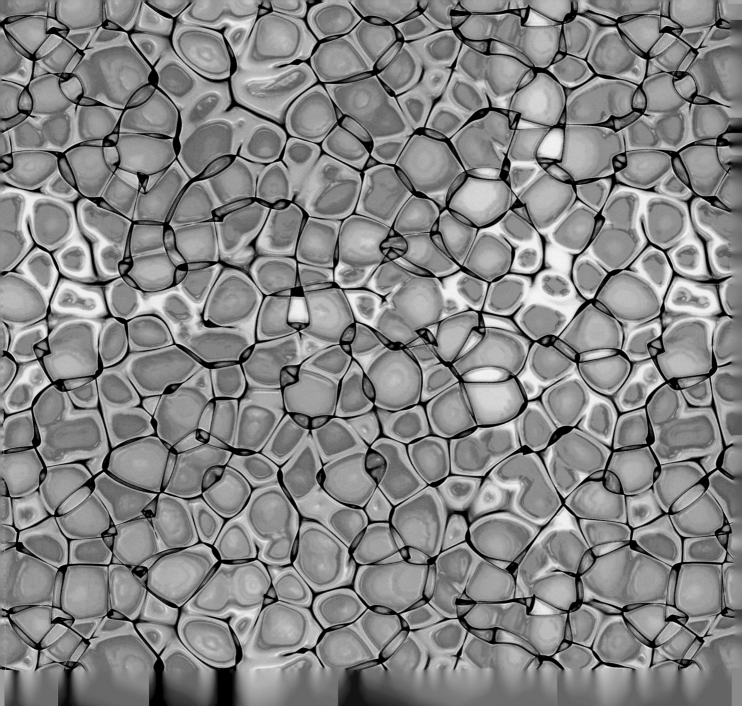

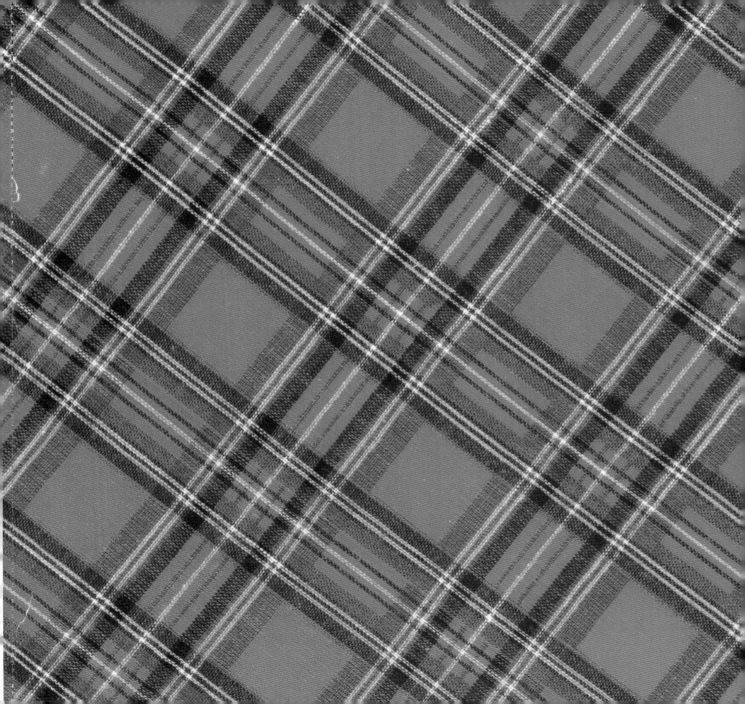

気前 GENEROSITY · 節奏 RHYTHM · 安全 SAFETY · 楽観 OPTIMISM · 音楽 MUSIC · 双子 TWINS · 梦想 DREAM · 奇蹟 MIRACLE · 金銭 MONEY · 希望 HOPE · 禁物 TABOO · 基督 CHRIST

壊滅 DESTRUCTION · 若死 DIE YOUNG · 夢魔 NIGHTMARE · 神意 PROVIDENCE · 変成 METAMORPHOSIS · 耶蘇 JESUS · 旅路 JOURNEY · 霊感 INSPIRATION · 変化 CHANGE · 絶望 DESPAIR

生命 LIFE · 智慧 WISDOM · 熱情 PASSION · 死亡 DEATH · 命運 DESTINY · 真相 TRUTH · 勇気 COURAGE · 進化 EVOLUTION · 诺言 FAITH · 愛人 LOVER · 永恒 ETERNITY

王子 PRINCE · 幸運 LUCK · 家庭 FAMILY · 信号 SIGNAL · 怪獣 MONSTER · 宇宙 SPACE · 星明 STARLIGHT · 星斗 STARS · 成功 SUCCESS · 自殺 SUICIDE · 和平 PEACE · 陽性 POSITIVE

頬笑 SMILE · 妬心 JEALOUSY · 月影 MOONLIGHT · 心得 KNOWLEDGE · 宿業 KARMA · 今日 TODAY · 友谊 FRIENDSHIP · 意力 WILL POWER · 哲学 PHILOSOPHY · 洋蘭 ORCHID · 沈黙 SILENCE

戦勝 VICTORY · 武者 WARRIOR · 兵士 SOLDIER · 美丽 BEAUTY · 寄波 SURF · 変幻 TRANSFORMATION · 復仇 REVENGE · 深潭 ABYSS · 悲劇 TRAGEDY · 革命 REVOLUTION

大安 LUCKY DAY · 冒険 ADVENTURE · 天使 ANGEL · 生変 BORN AGAIN · 極楽 PARADISE · 祝福 BLESSING · 堪性 PATIENCE · 欢喜 HAPPINESS · 快楽 PLEASURE

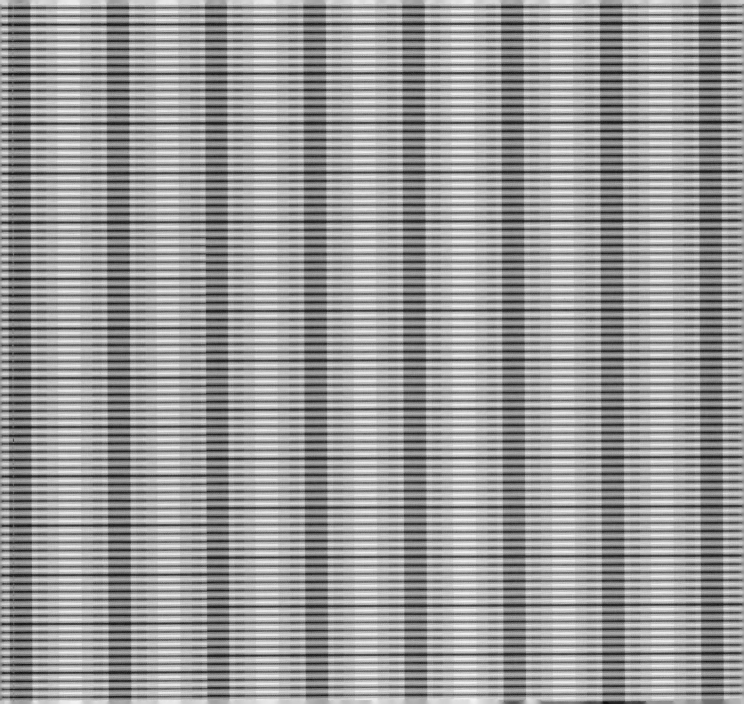

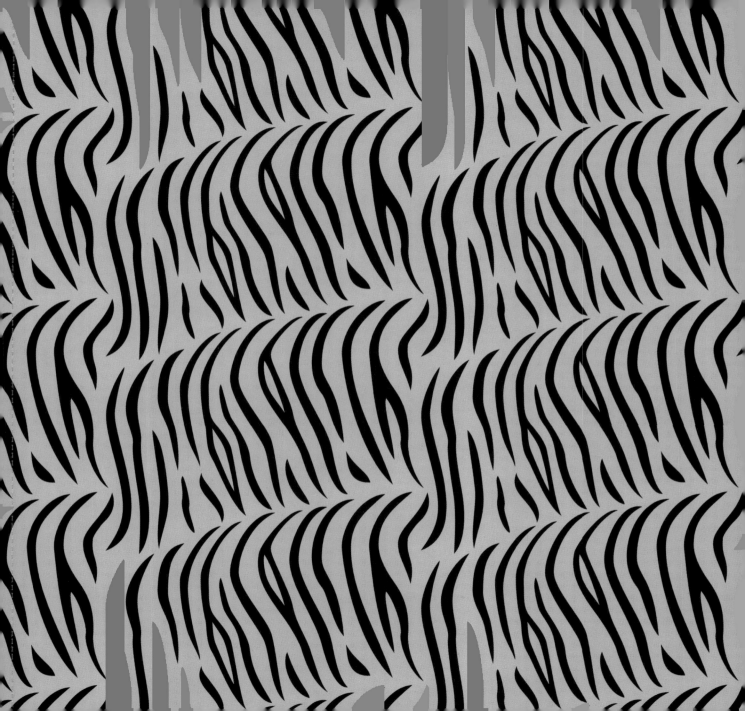

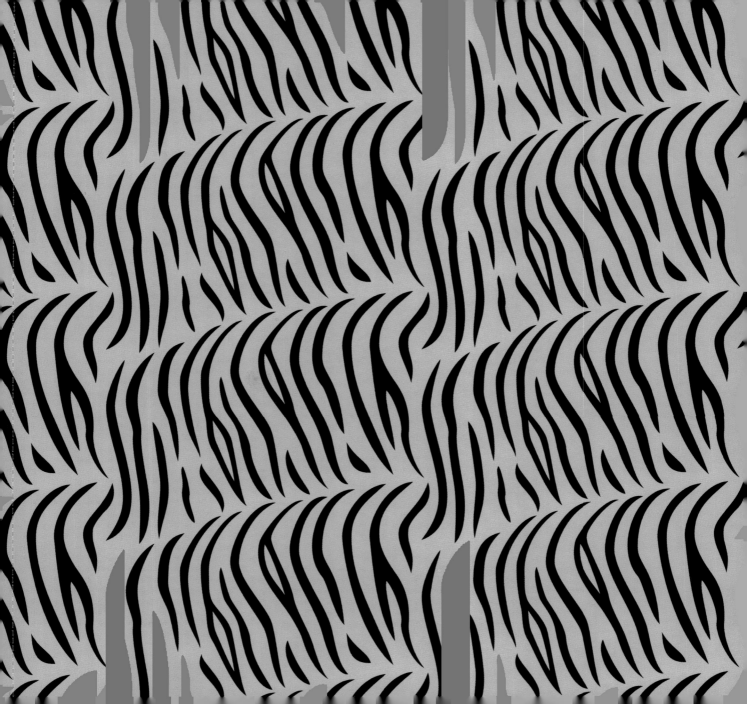

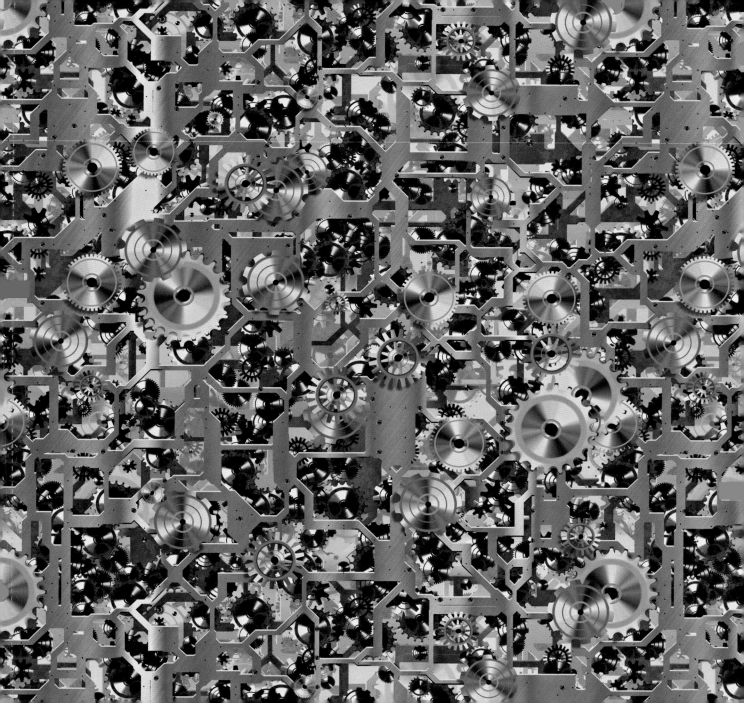

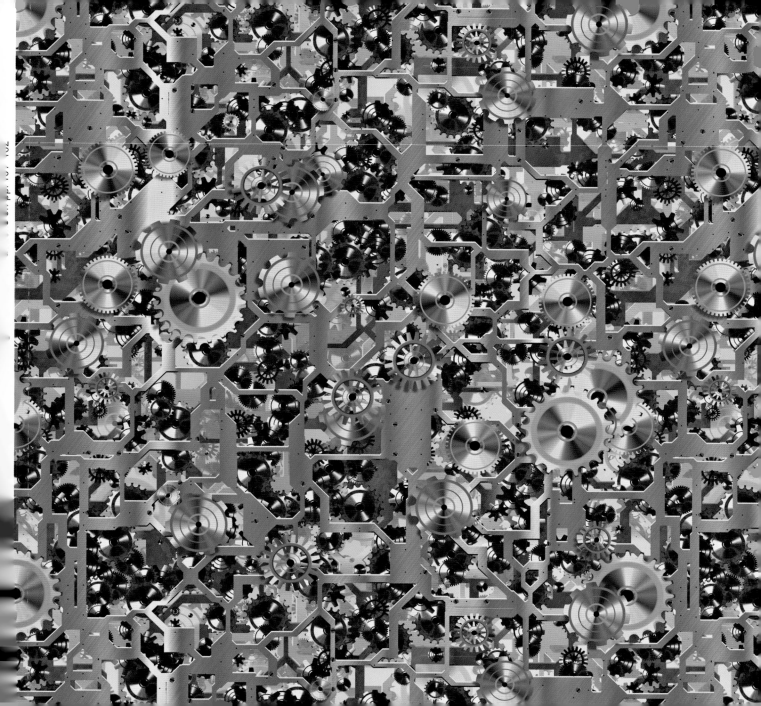

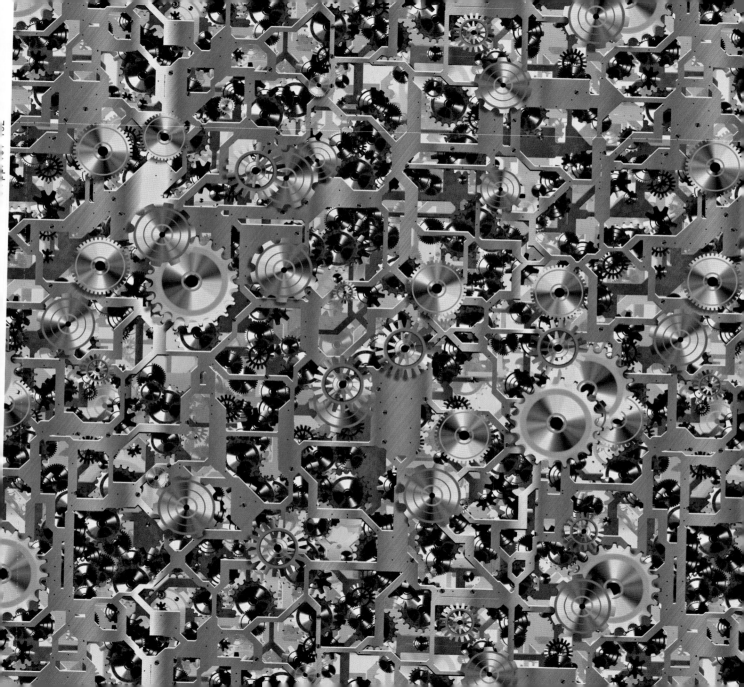

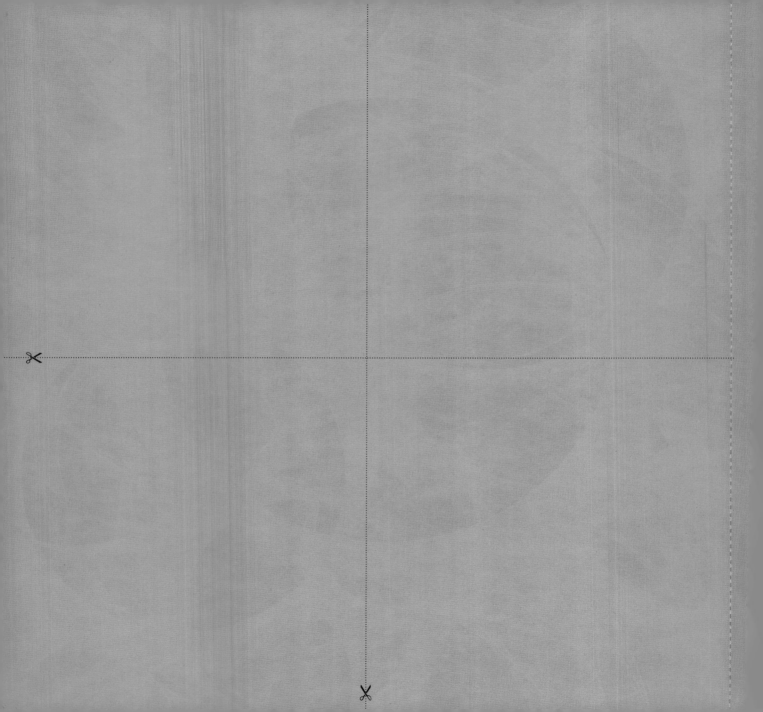

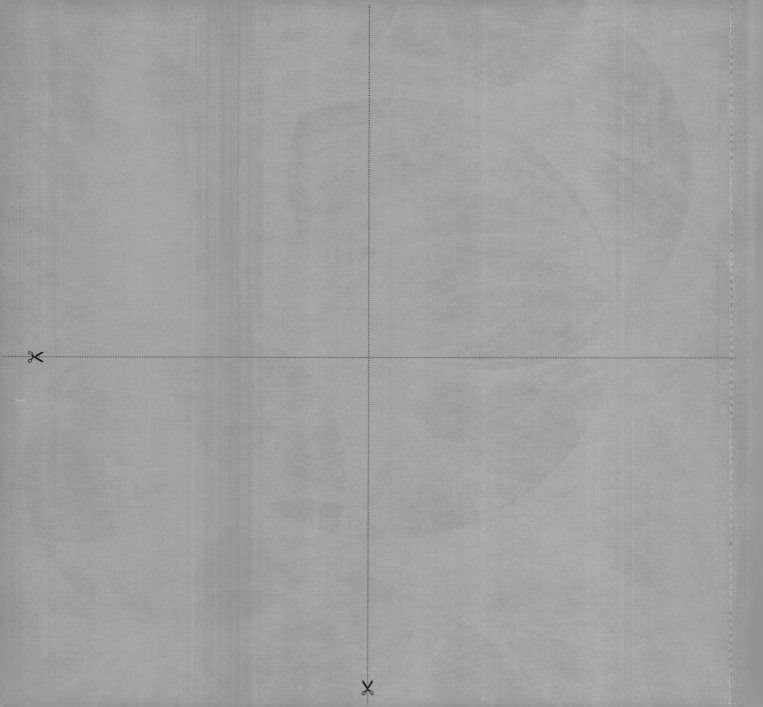

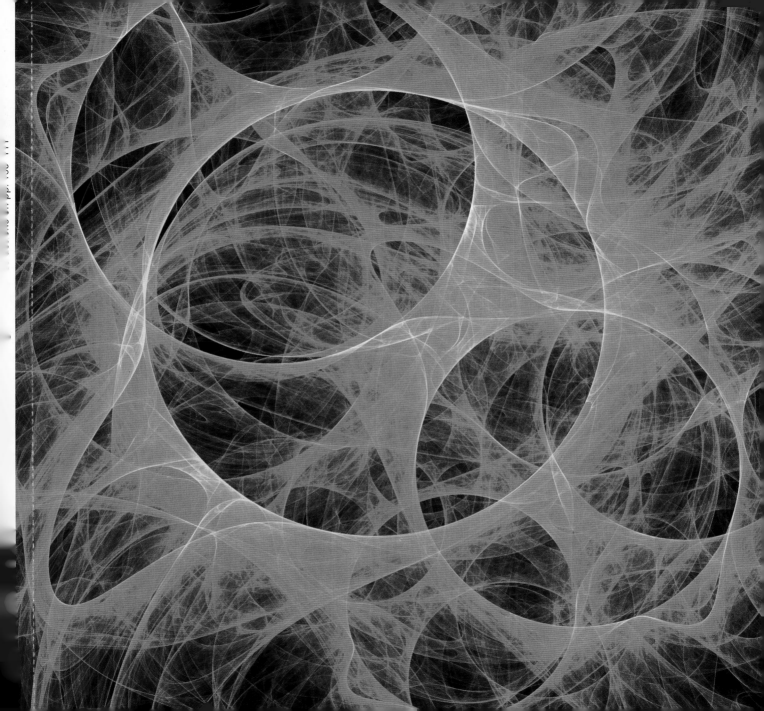

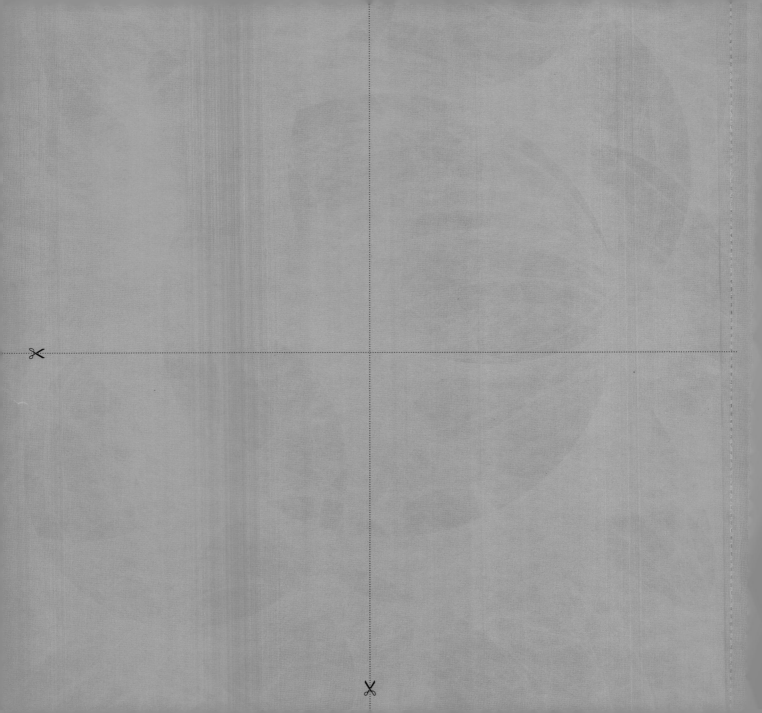

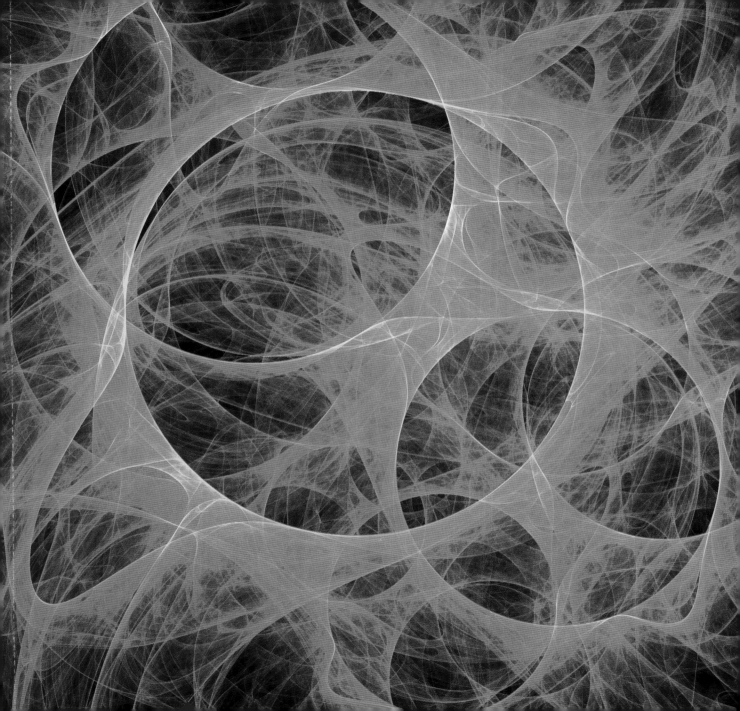

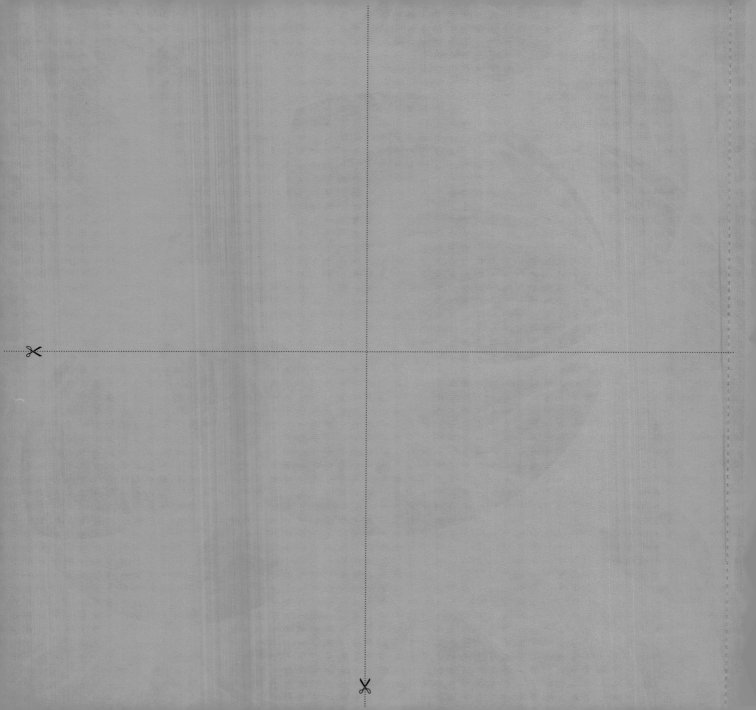

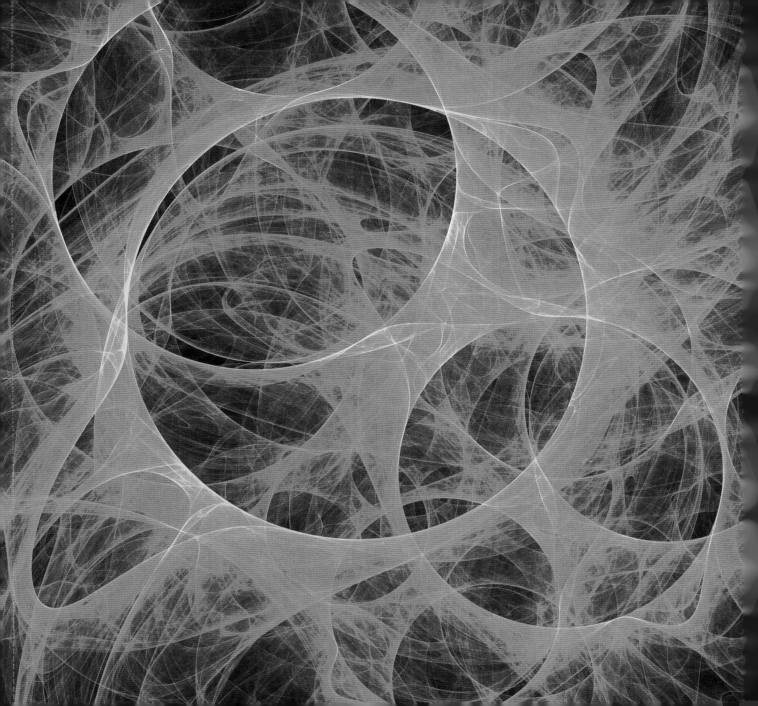

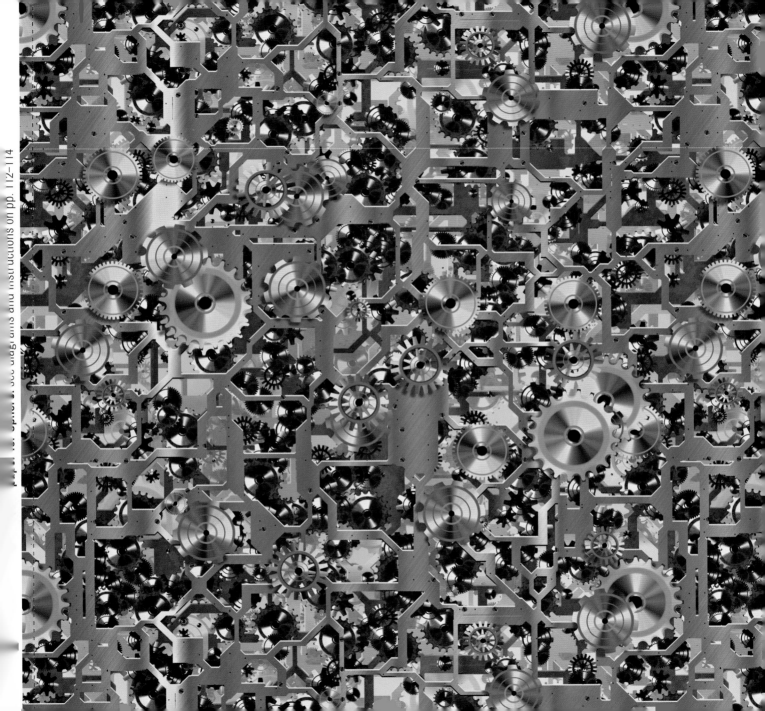

see diagrams and instructions on pp. 112–114

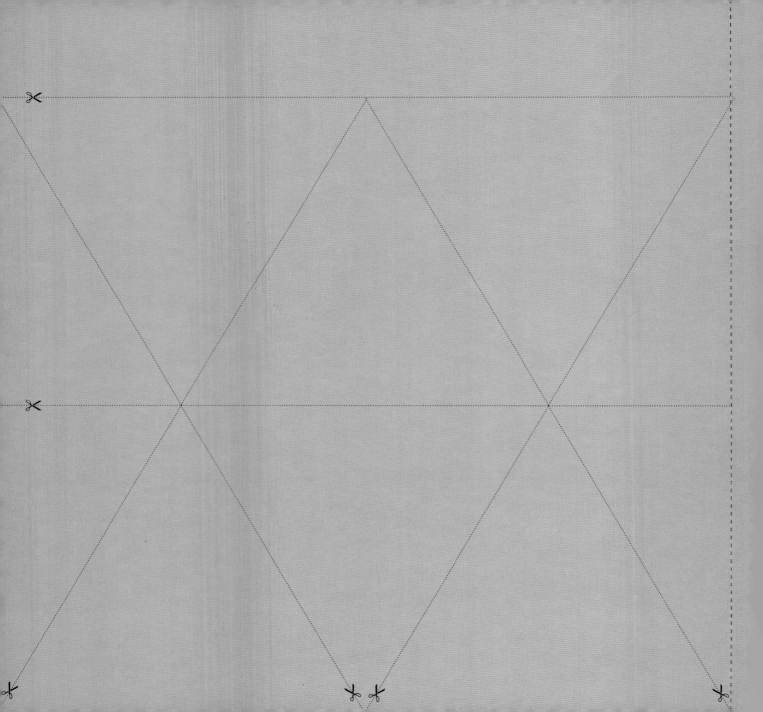

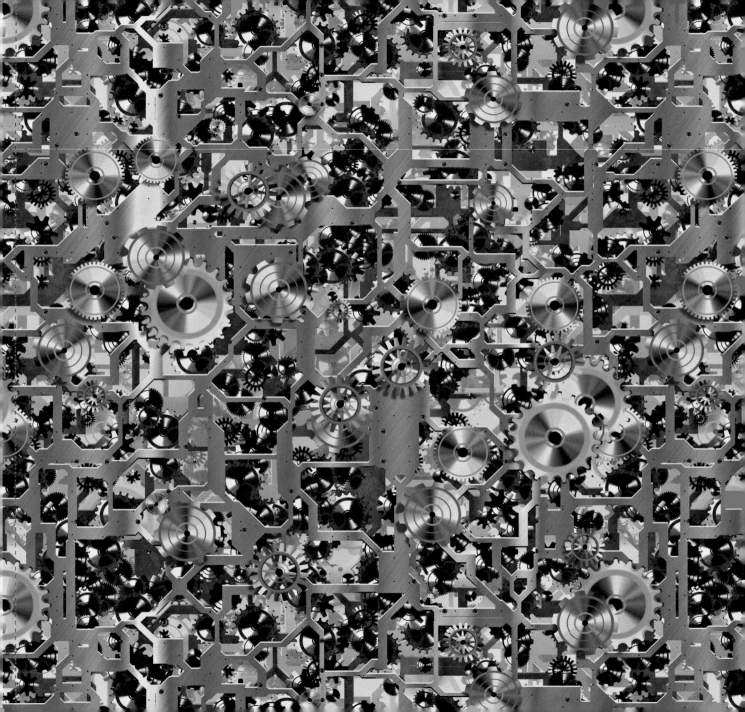

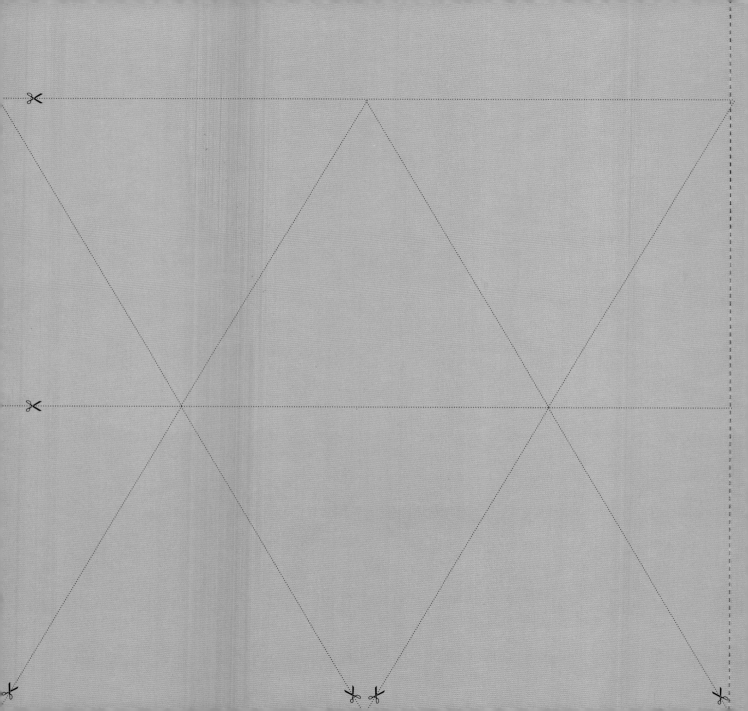

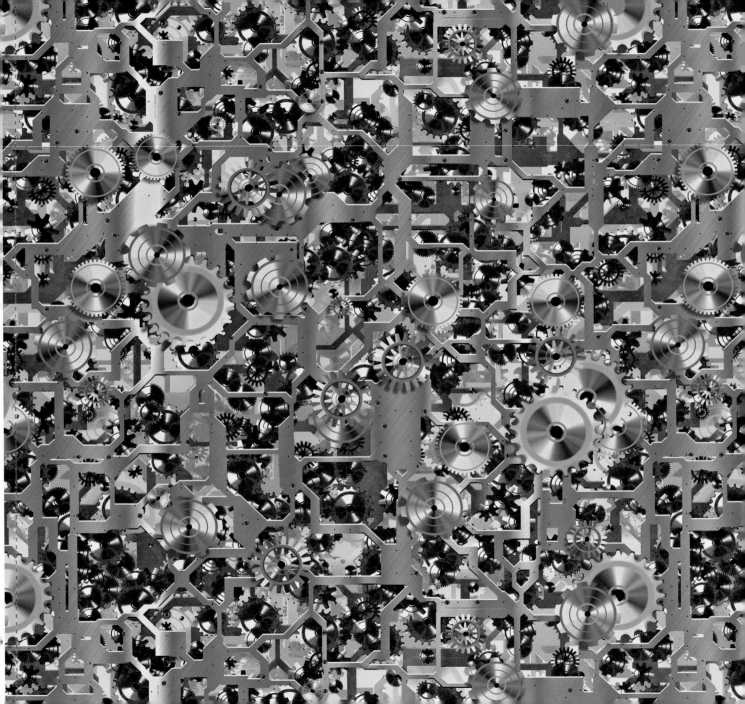

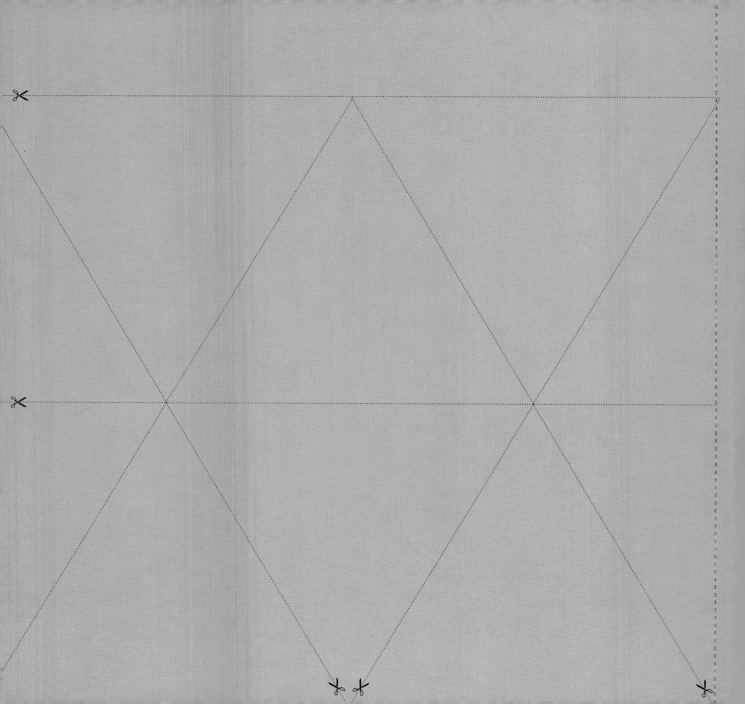

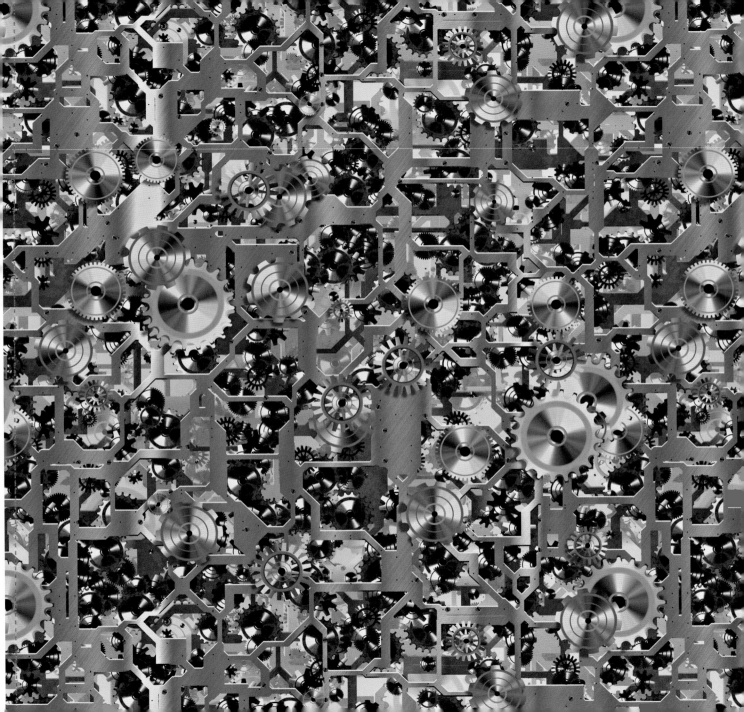

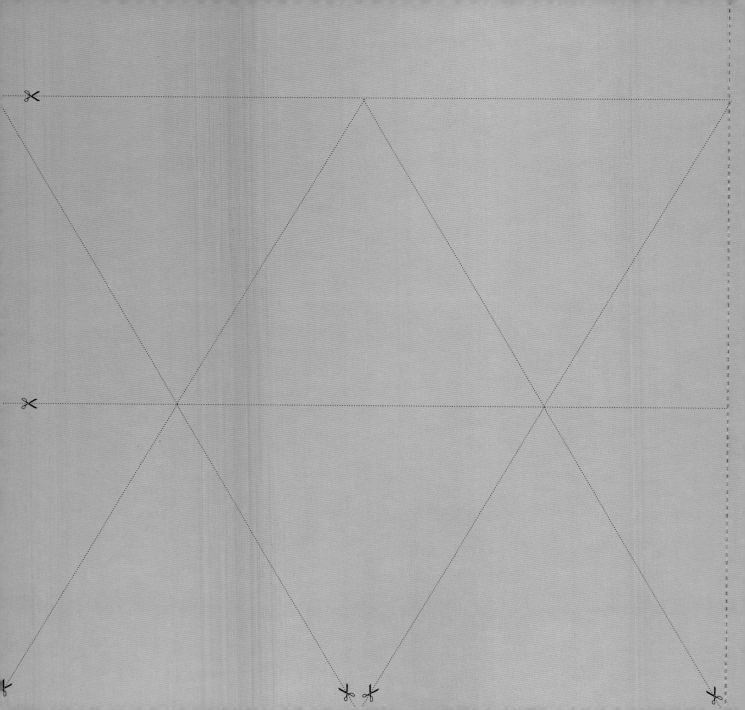

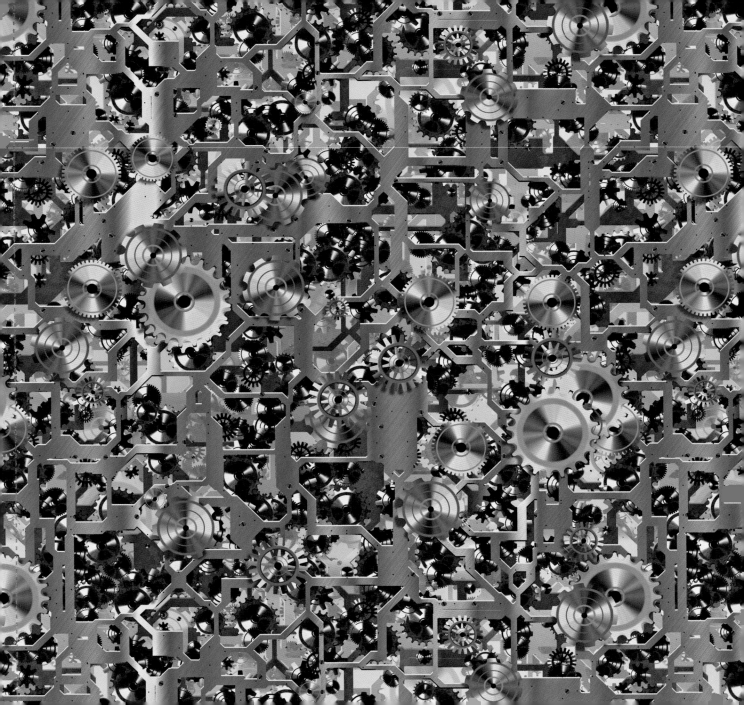

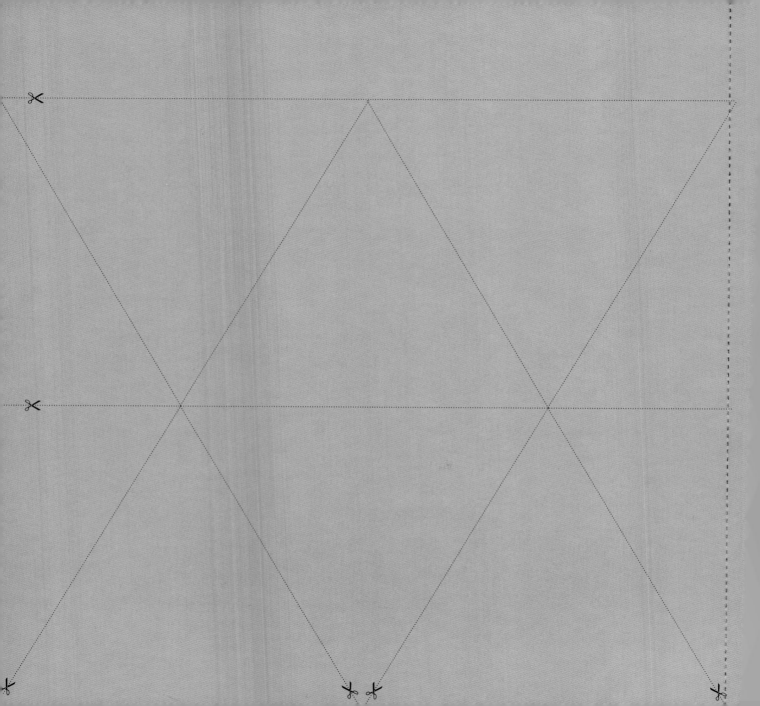

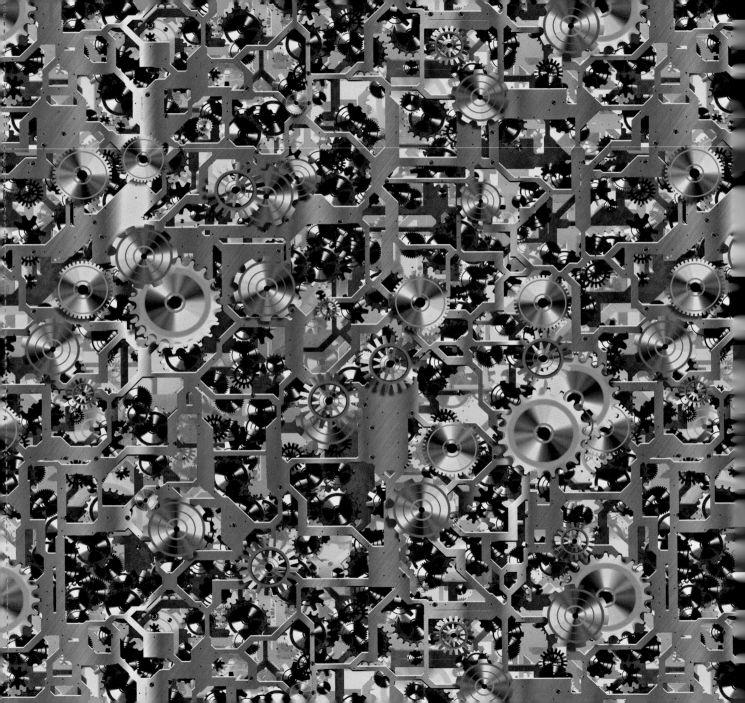

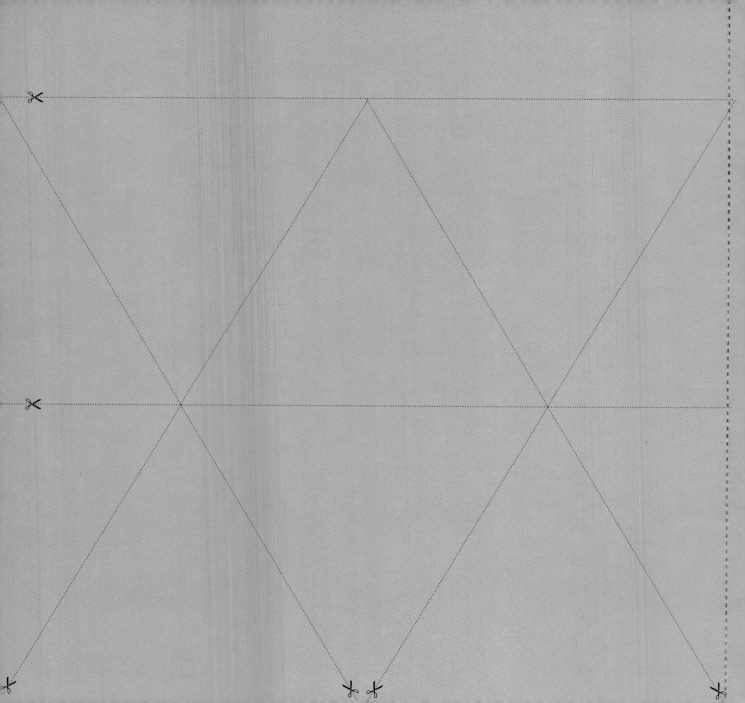

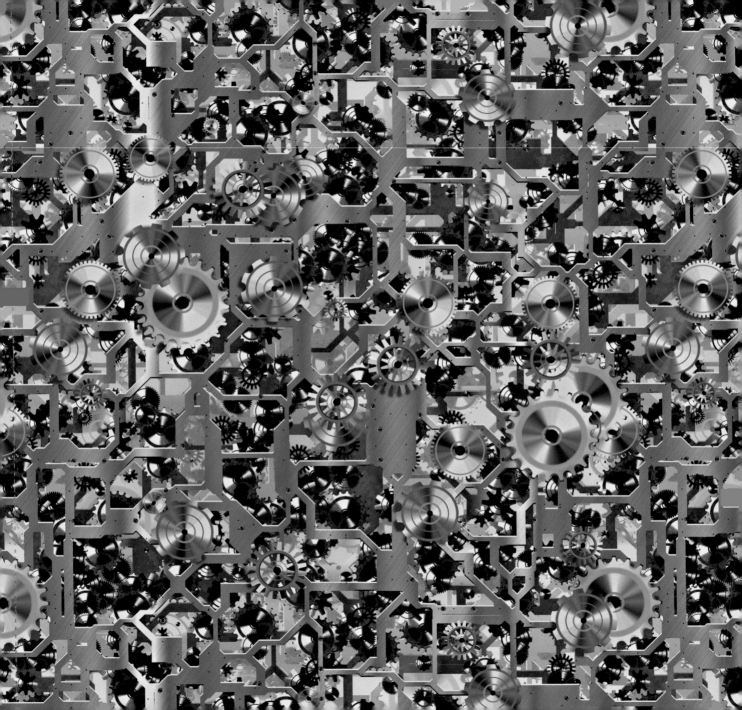

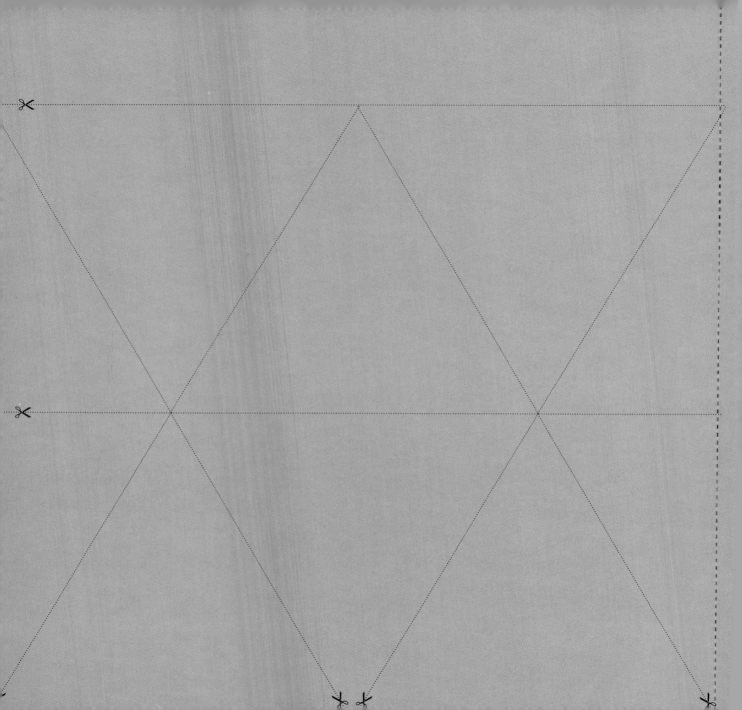

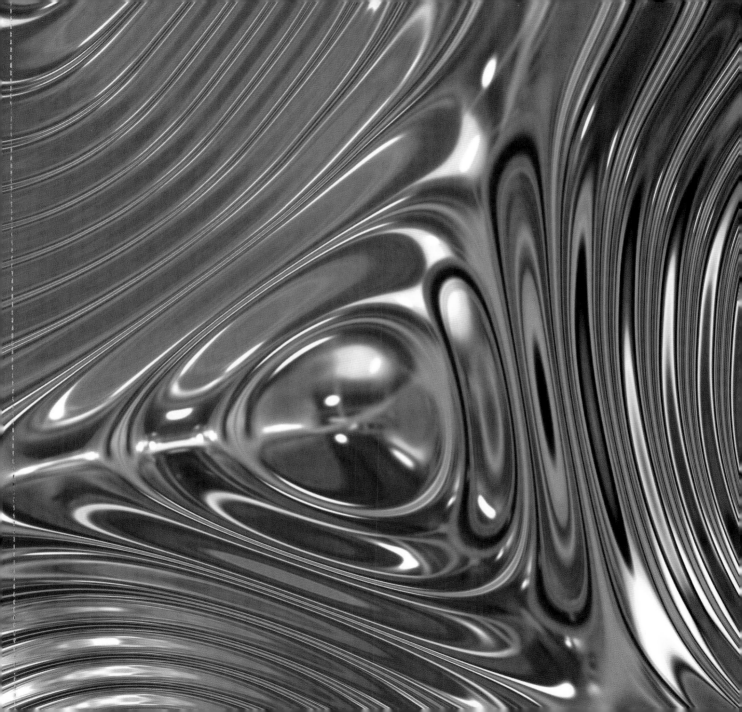

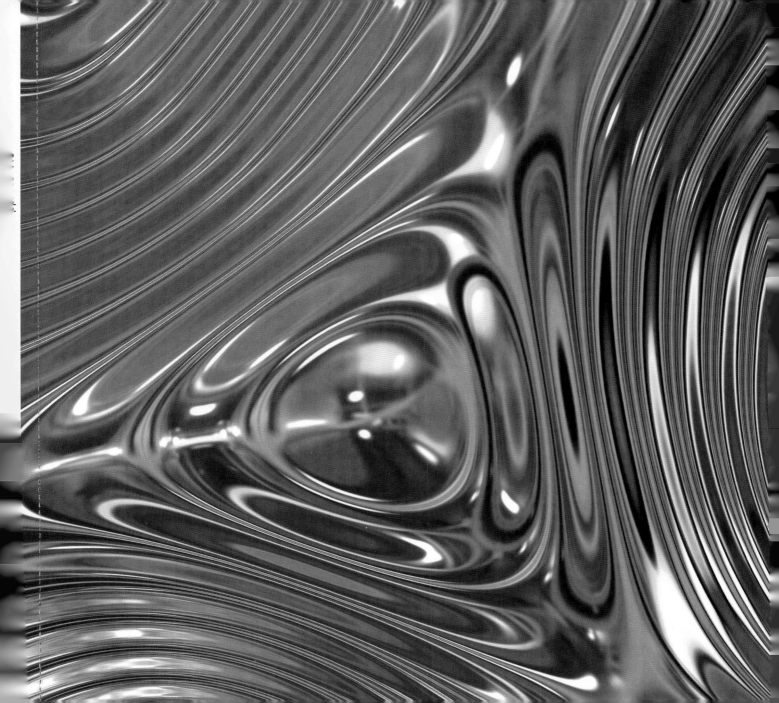